Success without Compromise

Richard H. LeTourneau

This book is designed for your personal reading pleasure and profit. It is also designed for group study. A leader's guide with helps and hints for teachers is available from your local Christian bookstore or from the publisher at $1.25.

VICTOR BOOKS

a division of SP Publications, Inc., Wheaton, Illinois
Offices also in Fullerton, California • Whitby, Ontario, Canada • London, England

Second printing, 1978

Unless otherwise noted, Scripture quotations are from
the King James Version. Other quotations are from *The
New Berkeley Version in Modern English* (BERK), ©
1969 by Zondervan Publishing House, Grand Rapids,
Mich., and *The Living Bible* (LB), Tyndale House
Publishers. All quotations used by permission.

Library of Congress Catalog Number: 77-80947
ISBN: 0-88207-757-0

VICTOR BOOKS
A division of SP Publications, Inc.
P.O. Box 1825 • Wheaton, Ill. 60187

Contents

Preface

All of us, particularly if we know and love the Lord, probably have developed an overriding drive in life that we feel a need to "get on with," especially as we get older. This need is not necessarily a life calling or an occupational position but is more related to a personal goal that we feel compelled to reach should the Lord allow us yet enough time to do so.

Some pastors or evangelists may have privately set a goal for the number of souls they would win to the kingdom of God. Others may have set a goal to see a certain organization established and running well. Some laymen may have set a certain dollar amount they would like to be able to feed into the Lord's work.

I have set such a goal too.

My goal relates to the testimony that my dad, the late R. G. LeTourneau, established in his lifetime. He proved that business and Christianity can work together. He then founded a college whose primary purpose was to give continuity to that testimony by training young people in the concepts of practical education and practical Christianity.

I know full well that both theologians and academicians tend to be theoretical in their writings and that available "practical" writings sometimes tend to be scarce. I also know full well that educational organizations tend to stray from their founding philosophy if there is not a very strong base of writings that commit them to the position intended by their founders.

With this in mind, my goal has been to get as much of this practical Christian academic philosophy into writing as possible, from as many different angles as I can come up with, to so firmly establish the position on which the college was founded that it really can't drift naively away from it. True, it can be changed by a future generation of the controlling trustee board. But if it is, it will need to be a blatant challenge to the values established, and everyone connected with it will know that its intended foundations are being destroyed.

Then, at the same time, if what I am doing can have an impact on Christians generally in Monday to Friday Christian living, I will be eternally grateful to God for the privilege of being a part of His work in this way.

This book is a part of my goal. It's the fourth (but I hope not the last) in the pursuit of establishing a base of practical Christian living and a framework of what I call "real" education for our young people.

The first (*Management Plus*) was aimed at developing a true leadership orientation in relationships with people and the accomplishments of goals.

The second (*Keeping Your Cool in a World of Tension*) was aimed at the need to keep a balance between the hilltop experiences and the nitty-gritty of everyday Christian living.

The third (*Success without Succeeding*) was aimed at equating faith with hard work in achieving success, both spiritual and secular, through a biographical narrative.

This book, (the fourth) is aimed at setting forth, in plain language, the elements of a practical lay Christian philosophy of life and work.

I dedicate this book to the faculty and staff of

LeTourneau College, both present and future, whose calling in life is to translate this practical Christianity into the lives of each succeeding generation until the Lord returns for His own. And my prayer is that the college will forever remain true to this founding philosophy as it is recorded in these and future works.

Introduction

"A layman has an advantage over the preacher. He has no ax to grind, no fish to fry." This is a familiar phrase to me for I've heard my father, R. G. LeTourneau, say it scores of times to audiences around the world during his thirty years of ministry as a layman for Christ. He would dare to broach subjects from the pulpit (such as money) that a pastor would be embarrassed to talk about so freely. And he would tell how God had blessed him in a successful business career.

Literally thousands of times during his lifetime he gave his testimony for Christ by "preaching" as a layman. As a faithful witness for Christ, he would leave his business on Friday or Saturday, fly to a distant city, give his testimony from three to eight times to various churches or groups, and then return Sunday evening late to continue his work as a diligent businessman for Christ as well.

One day he was explaining to a pastor why he thought people listened to laymen sometimes more than to the preachers. He said, "Most people feel that if a layman, who has the same day-to-day problems as they do, can make Christianity work, there must be something to it." Then he would add, "I'm not sure preachers don't have more problems than we do."

"Why of course we do!" the preacher responded emphatically. "I'm a paid salesman! You're a satisfied customer!"

There seems to be an insurgence of emphasis today on consumer information for the products and services available to us. This emphasis is frequently accompanied by a question on the merits of the advertising and selling claims to which we are so blatantly exposed on every hand. For years I have carefully followed the publications of various consumer testing organizations, as well as independent test reports, of products that appear in various publications. Why? Because of just what my father had said. I will listen much more carefully and with more confidence (and you will, too), to someone who uses this product or service, than to the manufacturer's advertisements. A user will tell me what may be good and what may be bad about the product since he is not connected with or paid by the manufacturer to do so. We assume that he, as Dad would say, "has no ax to grind or fish to fry," and we accept it as factual.

In Christianity I also see an insurgence of emphasis on this type of witnessing from the layman, from one who is really sold on what Christ has done for him personally, and is not being paid to talk about it. He, in effect, is giving a test report from a real-world application of the Gospel of Christ in his own particular situation. Since we, in listening to him, easily recognize this same applicability to our own lives, we are much more easily persuaded to accept this same Gospel as the guiding force for ourselves, too.

This book does not attempt to portray the flowery words or the emotional appeals of an advertising pitch or a television commercial to persuade you to try Christianity. It is, in essence, a consumer test report on Christianity as I see it, as I have observed it in my dad for over 40 years, and as I have lived it and tested it myself in the real business world, in the real educational world, and in the real world of various Christian organizations. It is designed to show you, in a real, practical way, how to live and breathe in the "rat race" world we find ourselves in, and be able to maintain our spiritual equilibrium while doing so.

Dad was a dynamic businessman. He was also quite expressive and demanding in his business when his workers didn't do things just like he thought they should have been done. Quite often he would exaggerate a condition or a mistake in order to call it to our attention more forcefully. When we would attempt to correct him on such an expansion of the facts, he would immediately catch himself; he would laugh and retort, "I'm just blowing it up a little so you can see it better."

As you read the various concepts which I have set forth in this book, and which I feel are very important to the layman in a "Consumer Test Report," I hope I don't offend your spiritual sensitivity in any of them. If I do perhaps you can obtain some comfort by saying to yourself, "He's just a chip off the old block. He's just blowing it up a little so we can see it better!"

I have not purposely done that, but I will allow you that much latitude of interpretation if you'll allow me that much latitude of presentation. Agreed? Fine! Let's get on with this analysis of how to survive the rat race without being unspiritual.

Part I One Way!

1

Are You Ready for the Race? And the Finish Line?

Over the years I have been fascinated by people who prepare for and run in track and field competition, particularly in the long distance races. Have you watched some of them in the televised reports of Olympic activities? If you have, you know from the expressions on the faces of the runners that it is grueling. The grimace and the anguish are obvious as they press with that last ounce of strength to gain on their competitor, or keep the competitor from passing them. And then that supreme last ounce of effort with every fiber of their being is thrust forth at the finish line.

Have you ever really tried to run a race like this yourself? I have tried (when I was considerably younger) but with little success. A few hundred feet and I was panting so badly and so many pains had developed that I'd have to knock it off.

How can these runners do what they do? Through training and preparation and setting their minds to the goal they are striving for.

I have a good friend who, when many of those around him began going soft and suffering heart attacks, decided that this was not for him and, well into his fifties, took up long distance running. Over the years following this decision he has run in dozens of marathon races, not measured in yards, but in miles—some twenty, thirty, or even fifty miles long. Now in his late sixties he still runs ten or fifteen miles just for warm-ups and to keep in shape. And he really is in shape—great shape.

But any doctor will warn you, even if you are in your twenties, not to try something like that without being prepared for it. The results could be disastrous. How do you prepare for long distance running? Will reading a lot of books on the subject help you? Not really! Will buying the right kind of sweat suit and good track shoes help you? Possibly some! Will eating the right kind of food do the trick? It could be part of it! But there is only one way to really prepare—train by running!

How did my friend, late in life, do it? He began by getting his body into shape physically and then starting out a few blocks at a time, then a mile or two, then longer. All at once? Certainly not! His conditioning and training took place over several years. So there's really only one way to prepare for long distance running and that is to follow a very precise and vigorous training schedule under the right kind of supervision. No other way will give you the ability to cope with the excruciating demands of the race before you.

There's another aspect of running a race that has interested me as I have observed it (from the comfort of my easy chair). Some will run a terrific race and be far ahead of their competition until that last turn in the track before the finish line, and then what happens? Someone lingering back in the pack, maybe even several runners back, who has paced himself properly and maybe in doing so has made only a mediocre showing up to that point—suddenly puts out a burst of energy and determination and comes sailing by the leader. And the leader, try as he might with a painful stretch of almost his last breath, can't prevent himself from being overtaken—just yards from the finish line.

What happened? The winner had not only prepared himself for the physical demands of the race but he had also prepared himself for the finish line. He knew exactly how much energy he had available, and he paced himself, conserving some of it until at a point he knew he had just enough left to give it all that he had and have no more to give, win or lose, when he reached that line.

Like preparing for a race, there's only one way to prepare for the finish line. You've got to pace yourself according to the length of the race and not run out of steam as the first runner did, just when he needed it most.

Life is also a race. We must prepare for it and be ready to meet the demands that it will make of us. We must also prepare ourselves for the finish line, as well, and the demands that will be made of us at that time also. The Apostle Paul likened this life to a race nearly two thousand years ago.

"Know ye not that they who run in a race run all, but one receiveth the prize? So run, that ye may obtain. And every man that striveth for the mastery is temperate in all things. Now they do it to obtain a corruptible crown; but we an incorruptible. I therefore so run, not as uncertainly; so fight I, not as one that beateth the air: But I keep under my body, and bring it into subjection: lest that by any means, when I have preached to others, I myself should be a cast-away" (1 Cor. 9:24-27).

And not only must we be prepared for the race, and for the prize or the finish line, but there is only one way to do this and God's Word sets it forth very clearly. "For there is one God, and one mediator between God and men, the man Christ Jesus" (1 Tim. 2:5).

Like in track competition, the things that best prepare us for the race also prepare us for the finish line. If we are really ready for this life before us, we'll also be ready to meet Christ at the end of it, either when He returns in all His glory (and that may not be long, now) or when we get promoted to be with Him at the finish line of our life's race.

What is this one way to prepare for both of these events? By being born again as set forth in God's Word. There is no other way to prepare to run the race before you and be able to cope with it. And that's what this book is all about.

This is an individual matter with you alone, no one else really being involved. It's not a family matter or an organizational commitment either. Becoming a church member, being baptized, being dedicated, knowing the language, and all of these things are fine, except none of them is the starting point of this preparation. Before any of this can have any effect you must first be born again. The procedure is simple. Almost too simple for many people.

First, each of us must recognize that we are sinners and that we were all born that way. "For all have sinned, and come short of the glory of God" (Rom. 3:23).

Second, we must recognize that as sinners we deserve eventual death. "For the wages of sin is death; but the gift of God is eternal life through Jesus Christ our Lord" (Rom. 6:23).

Third, we must recognize that God loved us to the extent that even though we are sinners and God can't look on sin, He sent His Son, Jesus Christ, to die in our place for our sin. "But God commendeth His love toward us, in that, while we were yet sinners, Christ died for us" (Rom. 5:8).

Fourth, we must recognize that all we have to do is to accept this substitution that God has provided. We must call on God, believe what He has done and confess to all men that we have believed.

"That if thou shalt confess with thy mouth the Lord Jesus, and shalt believe in thine heart that God hath raised Him from the dead, thou shalt be saved.

"For with the heart man believeth unto righteousness; and with the mouth confession is made unto salvation. . . . For whosoever shall call upon the name of the Lord shall be saved" (Rom. 10:9-10, 13).

Then all that is necessary is to *do* it. You don't need a pastor; it isn't necessary to join a church (that can come later). You just need to recognize the four concepts above, believe that God will accept you, as you are, make your decision to accept His provision, and God will do it. "But as many as received Him, to them gave He power to become the (children) of God, even to them that believe on His name" (John 1:12).

Then begin telling someone else about it and you're on your way. You have the starting point. You now have the basic strength and power resource available to you for the race ahead. It is instantaneous. There is no waiting period nor any delay. From this point you can really begin to train and build something worthwhile in your life.

My parents have accomplished great things for the Lord, having established one of the greatest lay witnesses this country has ever known. Yet what they have done did not make the decision for me. It obviously helped in my training and my outlook on life, but the decision to accept Christ had to be my decision alone and a decision for which I bore the total responsibility.

Neither you nor anyone else can depend on family connections or family Christianity as the decision or starting point for your readiness to meet Christ. Neither can you depend on an organizational or church membership as your credential of readiness to meet the Lord. Each of us must accept Christ according to the plan outlined in God's Word, a plan which is very clear and unmistakable. Don't let anyone lull you into a false security of joining something or doing something other than this as the means or prerequisite for your salvation. Just like the footrace, no one else can do the preparation and conditioning for you. You must do it yourself as an individual.

Then if you are ready in this respect you must also get ready in the other respects by being about the tasks which God has given you to do in the life race ahead. That's what this book is all about— a "how to" book and a test report from the world of business, industry, education, and Christian organizations as seen through the eye of a layman.

There is also a finish line in life's race. Christ is returning. The Scriptures are clear on this. Are you ready for His return? Have you accomplished or are you making good headway in accomplishing the

work that He has given you to do? Have you prepared your personal life so that there is nothing between you and the Master? I won't say that this has
always been true in my life. I have failed Him many
times, but I have asked His forgiveness when I have
failed Him and I continue to ask it when I fail Him
now. Being ready personally to receive the King
of kings on His return without embarrassment or
shame should be the goal of every born-again believer. It's the finish line that we're preparing for.

But let me carry this yet one step further. Some
years ago my wife and I were challenged greatly
by listening to a message from Hal Lindsay, author
of *The Late Great Planet Earth* and many other
books dealing with the return of Christ. When we
returned home that evening we began to ask ourselves, "What would happen to the material goods
and money that we have accumulated if the Lord
should return tonight?" Our first reaction was that
if we should be caught up in the Rapture, what we
left behind would go to our children or to Christian
organizations. Then it dawned on us that our children all know the Lord and they would go with us.
It also dawned on us that the Christian organizations to which anything else would be left would
also be disbanded (or should be) if they're worthy
of getting our money.

It was only then that we realized that should the
Rapture occur, any material goods or money that
we had accumulated would be left to the state or
to unsaved relatives. We began to ask ourselves, "Is
this what we are accumulating money for, to leave
to the state and to unsaved relatives?" Our resources
and material goods had been dedicated to God.
How could we possibly think of letting them end up
in this manner when we currently have full control

over them and can put them to work in Christian organizations to assist in winning souls to Christ and educating young people for service for Christ while there is yet time before the Rapture.

Of course, God expects us to be prudent and to provide for our own. I'm not saying that we should sell everything and give to the church or Christian organizations. What I am saying is that we need to keep the right perspective on the accumulation of wealth or savings so that we neither allow it to lie unused when it might win souls, nor allow it to become the nest egg in which we are trusting rather than in God. This, too, is part of being prepared for the finish line of our race.

Are you ready in terms of personal salvation? Are you ready in terms of a closer walk with the Lord? Are you ready in terms of putting your maximum resources to work for the Lord? You, there! Yes, you! I'm talking to you—no one else! Are you ready for the race and for the finish line? "Behold, I come as a thief. Blessed is he that watcheth, and keepeth his garments, lest he walk naked, and they see his shame" (Rev. 16:15).

Part II Two Buts!

2

But That's Not Being Spiritual!

A few years ago, I attended the annual convention of a church denomination attended by about 1,500 delegates, mostly pastors. One of the pressing issues to be decided was a reorganization of the administrative structure of the denomination to permit it to function and make decisions more efficiently. To do so, however, they needed to employ more business methods and to delegate more decision-making power to individuals rather than to reserve it for committees and for debate and discussion at an unwieldly session of 1,500 people such as was currently taking place.

I listened intently to a very disturbing line of arguments against the change. Not only were there many very vocal individuals against the change (it would have eliminated their "say-so" in many minor and procedural matters) but their basis for being against it didn't make sense. At least, to me it didn't.

They argued that we shouldn't have more order and efficiency (with greatly reduced cost of operation) because such worldly "management" methods would not allow sufficient room for the Holy Spirit to work within their midst. They were afraid that these worldly methods would "create a lack of cohesion among us and not allow the presence of Christ to be effective among us."

Their assumption told me that they felt the Holy Spirit could not lead dedicated individuals, only larger groups.

It was ironic. I would have been tempted to laugh if it were not so serious a matter. What was patently obvious to me was that the lack of good order, system, and good management procedure in the organization was certainly creating a lack of cohesion at that moment. And from the tone of some of the voices from the floor of the convention, neither could I detect the presence of Christ or the Holy Spirit guiding their remarks.

Many fail to recognize that our God is a God of order and efficiency. That does not mean He will not tolerate disorder or inefficiency, for He often uses it to work out His plan, but His first choice for us in almost any situation certainly cannot be disorder and the waste of the funds or resources that are available to us for His work. I'm convinced that many unsaved persons are turned away from the Gospel and that many unchallenged Christians are turned away from a life of service when they observe the costly, wasteful, and disorderly manner in which many Christian affairs are conducted. Paul set the tone for this in his message to Titus "that thou shouldst set in order the things that are wanting" (Titus 1:5).

There are, of course, occasions involving worship, as when Mary poured the costly ointment onto the feet of Christ (John 12:2-8). Her offering couldn't be considered waste, and neither should building an appropriate place of worship that is respectful and conducive to worship as long as its ornateness is not excessive. Basically the waste and inefficiency with which I am dealing is that which really does not contribute to an attitude of worship, but is where the worshipful surroundings are used as an excuse or a cover-up for pride or apathy.

In the denominational meeting to which I referred, the more efficient management system recommended would have meant less voice or input from the individual delegates in the day-to-day operational matters. It appeared to me that these delegates were not so concerned about the Holy Spirit being eliminated from church decisions but seemed to be more concerned that they personally would be excluded. Their rationale seemed to be that the Holy Spirit needed the voices of a large number of people, including themselves, through which to make decisions rather than making these decisions through guiding a few people involved in a more efficient management of affairs. This didn't make sense to me (and still doesn't). The Scripture is clear that we are to pay attention to our work and the cost of it.

"Wherefore, beloved, . . . be diligent that ye may be found of Him in peace, without spot, and blameless" (2 Peter 3:14).

"Seest thou a man diligent in his business? he shall stand before kings; he shall not stand before mean men" (Prov. 22:29).

Some years ago in visiting with an organization that was conducting research into missionary methods and effectiveness so that money could be spent more wisely in winning souls, I was told that they had faced a strong reaction from many of the missionaries. It seems that the missionaries couldn't conceive that an analysis of their work using statistics and a computer could show how they could be more effective. They were horrified at the thought that a computer could compile information sent in by them and tell them how to do their work better rather than relying on the Holy Spirit to guide them.

Before going further, let me point out that a computer is nothing but a high speed adding machine. All a computer can do is gather and sort information which is given to it. It cannot analyze or think beyond the powers of those who program or feed input to it. Its only function is speed, performing in seconds what might take years to do otherwise.

God expects us to use common sense in our work for Him. He expects us to analyze the effectiveness of this work. He expects us to minimize the cost and maximize the effectiveness of what we are doing. Few would question this concept. But when we attempt to do it faster at less cost, with a computer, this seems to create problems for some people.

In this sense, is using a computer any different than using a typewriter instead of handwriting all of our letters? Could not the Holy Spirit speak through us more clearly while we are handwriting a letter than He could while dictating or typing it? Possibly so. But I don't see too many Christians hung up on using a typewriter.

The same would be true of using a telephone instead of mail service, or using a car instead of walking, or using an airplane instead of a car or bus. It even applies to the use of television and radio instead of restricting ourselves to the people that we can gather within the sound of our voice.

Technology itself is not bad. God created technology and He expects us to use it for Him, to achieve the maximum results at the least cost as we look to Him for guidance.

There are skills in management just as there are skills in carpentry, typing, or any other manual profession. Many activities in Christian organizations and churches could greatly benefit from some of these skills in handling their affairs in a more businesslike matter. The use of these management skills in these organizations which are dedicated to God and guided by the Holy Spirit, is essential if we are to avoid discrediting Christ or Christianity in the eyes of others. Many may feel that to fail in using these skills is to waste the dollars entrusted to the Church and to give a false impression of what Christianity is all about.

3

But I'm Only Accountable to God! Oh Yeah?

After a lengthy discussion at a regular monthly meeting of the church governing board, a vote was taken. Contrary to the pastor's stated wishes they voted to order only 80 subscriptions to the denominational monthly magazine instead of the usual 120 subscriptions. The church treasury was unusually low and the board felt that the funds should be conserved.

The pastor had argued for the larger number so that he could distribute extra copies in the community, but the vote was taken and he was denied the extra copies.

Several weeks later, I learned that the very next day, this pastor submitted his usual order for the larger number and it was duly paid for by the church treasurer. His logic? He is responsible to God, not to man. He felt God wanted him to have the extra copies, so he ignored his accountability to his board and ordered them anyway. Was he right in what he did? Or wrong? This is such an insignificant example that you might be tempted to say, "Who cares?" But there is a very sound principle involved, and I purposely chose a picky example to make my point even more clear.

As Christians we are responsible not only to God but to man in various ways. To not be accountable to man for the ethics of our job or our business is to betray our Christianity and thus not be accountable to God either. Many of us operate in a gray area in the matter of accountability. Accountability is the requirement of doing something because someone else is expecting us to do it and as the dictionary states it, "The quality of giving a satisfactory statement of or explanation of one's conduct and obligations; being subject to an authority that may punish default."

It is really the quality of being able to follow through or to accomplish that to which we have previously made a commitment. It can be related to a person, to an organization, or to a principle or a philosophy. It may also be related to time, to money, or to the effort we expend. When we commit ourselves to something or somebody, and then don't follow through on that commitment, we have damaged our accountability.

The pastor I referred to made a commitment to the board of the church when he accepted the call to be its pastor. While he may have had good reason to negate his accountability in matters where spiritual principles were involved, he was definitely out of order in ignoring the financial and procedural directives of his board.

We make commitments every day. We made a commitment to God to obey Him and His Word when we accepted His provision for us. We made a commitment to our employer to perform our job to the best of our ability when we accepted that job and the paychecks that go with it. We made a commitment to a customer that our product or service was what we had said it was when we completed the transaction and accepted his money. Our accountability in each case depends on how well we honor these commitments. It is important for Christians to be what we say we are, to act like we say Christians should act, and to do what we say we will do.

"Every idle word [or deed] . . . they shall give account thereof" (Matt. 12:36).

"Unto whomsoever much is given, of him shall be much required" (Luke 12:48).

"Everyone of us shall give account of himself to God" (Rom. 14:12).

Colleges are monitored very closely by accrediting associations to make certain that they are held accountable to the public whom they serve. In my experience with the associations, I have found that they do not always tell us specifically what we should do or what we should be as a college. If there is one theme that they harp on consistently, however, it is that we must be what we say we are in our catalog and we must do what we say we will do as we represent ourselves to the public. To be accountable to the academic world, we must represent ourselves truthfully. The same is true with our spiritual foundations. If we claim to be a Christian college, or if we claim to be Christians, to be accountable we must build the college or our lives on the spiritual foundations of God's Word.

But we are human and we rationalize. We excuse ourselves by saying that in most cases it really doesn't matter, or we say that everyone else is doing it. We see another Christian doing something that is contrary to God's Word, and we adjust our standards temporarily so that we can do likewise.

When our fellow worker "borrows" material or supplies from the job, and even the boss turns his head, since everyone says the company "expects" this to happen, we say it must be all right. And when our competition forces us to misrepresent our product or service, just so we can compete and stay in business, we rationalize that, too, and say it is expected in the business world. But it is not!

We are accountable to God in obedience, in relationship to Him and in the way we conduct ourselves in our daily lives. We are also accountable to man to perform our job according to these same standards.

Stealing time from an employer by "goofing off" on the job, or by taking too long a coffee break, is no different than stealing money since we are paid money for the time we have lost. And when we do, we are not being accountable. We are operating in this gray area.

When a pastor says he is accountable to God, not to the board of his church, in matters of procedure or finance, he too is not being accountable. Each board member is accountable to God for these matters himself and when the pastor accepted that position he made a commitment to both the board and to God. This commitment was to God for spiritual principles, and to the board in matters of procedure and finance. When this is violated, he also is operating in a gray area.

Then, if we really want to make ourselves accountable, it may be necessary for us to even go well beyond that to which we have made a commitment.

In the late 1930s, when my dad was giving his

testimony in Nebraska one weekend, he shared the platform with Dr. R. A. Forrest, President of Toccoa Falls College, a small Bible college in the hills of northeast Georgia. Dr. Forrest was taking a sabbatical leave and was just leaving on a tour of the world, visiting the missions with which the graduates of his Bible College were serving. Dad was so impressed with Dr. Forrest that, after the service, he gave him a check for $1,000 asking him to use it "where it would do the most good." Dad promptly forgot about it, not anticipating to hear anything further in regard to it.

Several months later he received in the mail a large bundle of receipts accounting for every dollar and the cause for which it had been spent. Not one cent had been used for expenses; all of it had been given to various missionaries on his trip, and Dr. Forrest had insisted that each one give him a written receipt that he could send back to Mr. LeTourneau as an accounting for the gift he had given. You may ask, "Why did Dr. Forrest go to so much trouble when it wasn't asked for or expected? What did he gain by it?"

That single act of accountability so impressed my father that he decided to check further into such a man who could be that trustworthy and that businesslike. The result? Over the next thirty years or so following this incident, several hundred thousand dollars were given to that little school to help in its ministry. In addition, Dad built a new factory near the school and hundreds of students were given an opportunity to work, earning an education which they could not have afforded otherwise. Hundreds of millions of dollars were pumped into the economy of that northeast Georgia community over a period of years. The man who was so trustworthy and accountable had initiated this remarkable chain of events.

Let's show the nonbelievers with whom we work and associate what real accountability is—to God as it relates to scriptural principles and scriptural commands—and then to man also as it relates to the hierarchy of authority and the ethics of our profession within which we have made our commitments.

Part III Three Challenges

4

Sometimes It Takes Guts to Make a Decision

Years ago a staff member in one of my dad's plants was offered an opportunity to move to a new plant that was being established in another part of the country. The decision was left up to him. After much prayer and frustration he still couldn't make up his mind. Finally someone else decided for him and transferred him to the new operation. Later, when he was offered an opportunity for an advancement, the same thing happened. This time, however, he didn't get the expanded responsibilities.

In my own association with this man I began to notice this same characteristic in the little things also. It would take him literally months to buy a new car or to decide on a house to live in. Even where to go on vacations proved a real dilemma.

He was a very spiritual man and trusted God a great deal, but he seemed to have trouble in getting clear signals from God. He was indecisive about almost everything.

But shouldn't we seek God's guidance on everything we do? Yes, certainly! But God provides His guidance in many ways, including the circumstances He puts us in and the common sense He gives us. The late Dr. A. W. Tozer expressed this clearly in his tract, "How The Lord Leads."

On the surface it appears more spiritual to seek God's leading than to just go ahead and do the obvious thing. But it is not. If God gave you a watch, would you honor Him more by asking Him for the time of day or by consulting the watch? If God gave a sailor a compass, would the sailor please God more by kneeling in a frenzy of prayer to persuade God to show him which way to go, or by steering according to the compass?

Dr. Tozer qualified this concept two ways, however. First, we must be born again and in close fellowship with the Lord. Second, doing the obvious thing shouldn't be contrary to spiritual commands as far as "do's" and "don'ts" are concerned. Beyond that, we can trust God to give us the good sense to do what's right and depend on Him to create the circumstances that will open or close doors if we do make a mistake.

Many Christians go through life in a constant quandary, wondering about everything they do, including what breakfast cereal God wants them to eat or what color toothbrush they should buy.

If, as Dr. Tozer says, God is pleased when we are pleased, as long as we meet the basic requirements for guidance, then why should we be so indecisive? Christians more than non-Christians should be able to make decisions when necessary without fear of the results, knowing that God will make it turn out so that it was the right one or else He will stop us cold in our tracks and turn us another way.

God's Word gives us two examples of people not wanting to make a decision and who were lost as a result. The man who came to Jesus seeking eternal life didn't have the guts to make a decision for Jesus because he had too many possessions.

Then Jesus beholding him loved him, and said unto him, "One thing thou lackest; go thy way, sell whatsoever thou hast, and give to the poor, and thou shalt have treasure in heaven: and come, take up the cross, and follow Me." And he was sad at that saying, and went away grieved; for he had great possessions (Mark 10:21-22).

Elijah also had a problem getting people to make a decision for God:

And Elijah came unto all the people, and said, "How long halt ye between two opinions? If the Lord be God, follow Him: but if Baal, then follow him." And the people answered him not a word (1 Kings 18:21).

My dad was a very decisive man. He had very little patience with those who could not make decisions. As a result he had little patience with the man I referred to earlier and this man had to be dismissed later primarily because of his indecisive character. (He was out of work for several months after this, putting his family in a real bind. Even though he had several job opportunities, he just couldn't decide which one the Lord wanted him to take.)

Dad would admonish us regularly, "If you've got all the information you need to make a decision, then make it; don't put it off." He felt there was a time for prayer and consideration, certainly. He also felt there was a time for action. And he liked to see action when it was needed without the delays of "putting things off."

The difference between a successful manager or leader and one who is unsuccessful is largely in the area of being able to make decisions. A leader who won't make decisions is not much better off than one who makes wrong ones.

The problem with most of us is that we are afraid of making a wrong decision and are unwilling to live with the consequences of a wrong decision. Therefore we try not to make any decisions.

A leader knows he is going to make some wrong decisions. They just can't be avoided. He also knows, however, that if he makes enough right choices and learns how to cope with the wrong ones, he can move ahead while others are standing still in indecision.

Christians should have no such problem. We have the Holy Spirit available to guide us in all that we do. Perhaps we are like the automobile. As long as we are standing still, the Holy Spirit can turn our steering wheel in many different directions and nothing will happen. If we will make some decisions, however, and get moving, then He can turn our steering wheel and get us headed in the right direction.

Neither should we be afraid of the results of a wrong decision. If we are in a close walk with the Lord *all* things work together for good, including the decisions which we or others may have felt were wrong.

Trust in the Lord. Walk in close fellowship with Him. Be guided by scriptural commands. Then make the decision that looks right in the good sense He has given you. If He wants you to delay, He'll make that clear, too, but don't let your indecision be the result of your own fear of failure or your own lack of understanding about how God can guide.

5

Don't Infringe
on My Freedom

When I was in my late teens I used to ride a motorcycle quite a bit. It wasn't like the lightweight
Japanese bikes we see so many of today, but a big
heavy Harley-Davidson, 61 cubic inch, overhead
valve job, more like the police still use today. I've
got more sense now than I did in those days, but
it was great fun. A group of us even became proficient in standing up on its big wide seat, traveling
for miles without sitting down, steering by just
leaning slightly one way or the other. Our speeds
were slow and none of us ever fell off, but I certainly wouldn't recommend this to any sane human
being.

Motorcycles are licensed to use the streets and
highways under the same rules as automobiles.
They have the same rights and freedom as do automobiles. But because they are smaller and are sometimes unseen by other motorists or not given a full
traffic lane by others, a special danger is present
for these bike riders. If you've ever ridden one you

probably learned quickly a technique known as defensive driving. This means that if someone else wants to infringe on your freedom of the road, you let him. You even try to anticipate when someone else may attempt to infringe and you even welcome him to do it. Why? Because in a conflict with another vehicle, the motorcycle rider is always the loser, whether he has the right-of-way or not.

Christian freedom is a lot like that of a motorcycle rider. We have the right to do a lot of things that immediately become unwise to do, when we recognize that our spiritual lives are injured when someone else disagrees with our right to exercise that freedom.

Both Peter and Paul have some very specific advice on this matter of Christian freedom.

You are free from the law, but that doesn't mean you are free to do wrong. Live as those that are free to do only God's will at all times (1 Peter 2:16, LB).

You have been given freedom: not freedom to do wrong, but freedom to love and serve each other (Gal. 5:13, LB).

Freedom, particularly Christian freedom, is greatly misunderstood by many people. To many people, the concept of freedom means the ability to do as you please, without constraint of any kind and regardless of how it affects other people. Even if others are not considered, there is still no such thing as freedom, according to the definition that some would apply. Freedom by almost any definition really means the absence of *necessity* for constraint rather than the absence of constraint itself. This means operating within a realm and in such a manner that constraint is not necessary to be applied.

This is true in the physical world around us. The laws of gravity, the laws of inertia, the laws of forces all come into play in almost everything that we do. As long as we operate within the limits of these laws we can have freedom of physical movement but immediately when we attempt to go outside these laws, our freedom ceases.

For example, you can't have "freedom" in driving a car if you need to constantly keep reminding yourself of every function of the car, the rules of the road, and where all other drivers are going. No, you learn to drive and become so familiar with your car, with traffic laws, and with other drivers' reactions that you monitor and accept them without any conscious question. You then relax within the framework of protection and mobility that this experience gives you. When you have this kind of experience and attitude, you can have "freedom" in driving your car. You accept the limitations of your car, the circumstances around you, and the actions of other people. Then you are "free." You can get into your car, go down to the corner store or to the school and return without once giving serious thought to all the complexities of your car's operation, of traffic control around you, and of other drivers' actions. It becomes second nature to you. You are operating within the constraints or limits that apply. This is real freedom.

The same concept is true of a professional photographer operating a complex camera. He can use a great deal of "freedom" in its operation. It becomes second nature to him, yet he is hemmed in by myriads of restrictions and rules; if any one is broken he will fail to get the picture he really desires. But he has learned through hard experience what these are. He uses these restrictions to his advantage, subconsciously observing all the rules and the do's and don'ts that apply.

So real freedom is not "doing as you please." To do so might mean injuring or killing yourself or others, as in the case of the motorcycle, and possibly destroying property or at least failing to accomplish an objective. Real freedom can be summed up in two basic concepts.

1. *You maintain such perfect control of yourself and the affairs around you so that you do not operate outside the laws of God* (physical laws) *or the laws of man* (government and organizational restraints). When we have learned to so control what we do that we are not constantly bumping into these laws that must of necessity turn us in another direction, then we can indeed have freedom to control our own direction and activities. When you first learned to ride a bicycle you probably bumped into a lot of things, and undoubtedly caused injury to yourself and possibly others. Once you learned to control the bicycle within the laws of inertia, gravity, and centrifugal force, you probably became almost as "free as a bird" in operating that bike. This is the meaning of this first concept of freedom.

2. *You develop a sense of responsibility to self and to others* so as to avoid injury, whether physical, mental, moral, or social, and so that in the exercise of your "freedom" you do not interfere with or limit unnecessarily the freedoms of other people. The reason for stop signs and traffic lights for automobiles is not to periodically give your car a rest, but to so allocate the rights to cross an intersection that one person isn't interfering unnecessarily with another person's freedom. If traffic from both directions had freedom to move through a congested intersection, the obvious result would be either a

traffic jam or an accident, and in either case no one would have any freedom. (If you have ever driven a car in Paris or Mexico City you have a vivid impression of what I am saying.) So in order to retain the maximum amount of freedom for each person those rights must be allocated through the use of control devices such as stop signs or traffic signals.

Therefore, true freedom involves both control and responsibility. Control within the rules or laws that apply and responsibility to self and to others to minimize interference with other freedoms.

The freedoms available to a Christian, spoken of by Paul and by Peter, can be defined in almost precisely the same terms. God has established some rules, some guidelines, some do's and don'ts in Scripture to which we are commanded to adhere. As long as we maintain control of our lives and learn to live so that we are not continually bumping into these rules, we can have perfect freedom. But, like riding the bicycle, we must learn that there are certain things that Christians are not permitted to do. These things are forbidden in the Scripture; they are called sin. When we so learn to control our lives so that operating within the boundaries that God has set for us is second nature to us, then, and only then, can we have that freedom.

But as in physical freedom discussed above, there is also a responsibility involved in our Christian freedom. Not only must we maintain control of our lives so that we operate within the boundaries of God's law, but we must also operate in such a way that we exercise responsibility not to injure ourselves or others or take away the freedoms of others by what we do. In this sense, we must learn that "All things are lawful for me, but all things are not expedient" (1 Cor. 10:23) and that we should, "take heed lest by any means this liberty of [ours] become a stumbling block to them that are weak" (1 Cor. 8:9). Just as in exercising our freedom in driving a car we may restrict someone else's freedom, so we must exercise care and responsibility in the use of our spiritual freedom that we do not become a stumbling block to others.

In driving a car or riding a bicycle, we almost unconsciously obey the laws and responsibility involved because through our experience this has become second nature to us. The beauty of spiritual freedom is that we also have a second nature available to us through the Holy Spirit to help and guide us. We must, of course, maintain a close walk and communion with the Lord. We must study and learn so that we have the experience and judgment that is necessary. When we have done this we can rely on the Holy Spirit to give us that "second nature" that will allow us complete freedom while still maintaining perfect control and necessary responsibility.

6

Don't Be an Oddball

You could almost hear the gasp that went across the congregation of that staid old conservative church when, for their formal Sunday morning worship service, the young visiting evangelist walked out onto the platform in a bright red plaid jacket, red socks, and white two-tone shoes.

In contrast, the "Ohhhh, Noo!" was definitely audible at the Saturday night youth rally when the visiting missionary speaker appeared in black conservative dress that was definitely out of keeping with the audience he expected to reach.

The style of our dress or the clothing which we wear is not really important to most Christians, nor is it of great concern to non-Christians. But a few in both areas seem to have problems with types and styles of clothing. Few of the style changes in clothing could honestly be classified as unscriptural. Aside from some clothes which are purposely designed to be sexually revealing or stimulating, there are few scriptural do's or don'ts involved. There are some courtesy matters, however, which should be discussed and which can be important to the testimony of a Christian, both to fellow believers and to non-Christians.

Paul alludes to this type of influence that, I feel, can apply to our dress.

. . . that no man put a stumbling block or an occasion to fall in his brother's way (Rom. 14:13).

It is good neither to . . . [do] any thing whereby thy brother stumbleth, or is offended, or is made weak (Rom. 14:21).

Let every one of us please his neighbour for his good to edification (Rom. 15:2).

These verses apply to Christian courtesy relating to dress. While I would prefer to use positive terms, I think negative terms will give a clearer picture for these concepts. Here are five which a Christian should give careful thought to.

1. *Our clothing should not be unkempt in cleanliness or general appearance.* It should be at least as clean and in as good order as those with whom we generally live and associate. There is just no reason why a Christian should not be clean and neat in appearance. To be otherwise reflects unfavorably on his testimony and certainly does not make the Christianity to which he gives witness appear desirable to others. Obviously there are circumstances such as in work situations where this cannot always apply, but aside from those, cleanliness and neatness are important.

2. *Our clothing should not be offensive.* It should be appropriate or acceptable, culturally, for the circumstances whether it be a church service, a business meeting, a funeral, a sports event, or whatever. Different societies and different cultures have adopted unwritten standards as to what is appropriate and is acceptable. And a Christian should not

offend these standards if he is truly to have an impact with his witness.

3. *Our clothing should not be immodest when it can be modest in appearance or style.* In this one area clothing can become a scriptural problem if it is sufficiently immodest to be revealing or sexually stimulating. A good rule for Christians to follow is to keep styles on the conservative edge of what is acceptable in society when styles move in immodest directions. But not so conservative as to create problems in the next two categories.

4. *Our clothing should not be ill-fashioned when it is possible for us to be reasonably current in styling.* There are limits to this, of course, and each of us will need to determine where "fashion" and "modesty" collide and where the line must be drawn. I do not feel that this happens too often but here again this must be an individual judgment.

5. *Our clothing should not be attention getting in extremes of style, coloring, or materials.* While Christians should not be the oddballs in having old-fashioned clothing, neither should they be in the forefront of attracting attention so that they stand out in a group. There is nothing scripturally wrong in this except that the non-Christian has certain conservative standards which he thinks should apply to the Christian and to depart too far from them may cause harm to our testimony.

To put this over in the positive realm, we Christians should be fashionable, appropriate, conservative, and neat in our clothing and appearance so that we do not let ourselves (self) get in the way of our witness for Christ, and so that those to whom we are witnessing can see Christ only in the Gospel which we present.

Part IV Four Lessons

7

We Are Creatures of Habit

A friend of mine who lives closer to the church than most of the members and who has no children at home is almost always late for church services. He is also almost always the last one to arrive for a dinner invitation. Why? A habit! But this friend has other habits, such as always opening the car door for his wife or for other women and even men if it makes it more convenient for them. He is also courteous, gracious, and complimentary, with always a good word for everyone he meets. These are habits, too! But they are good ones.

Years ago, another friend of mine would almost always fall asleep during the morning worship service in our church and he was an elder of the church! Why? A habit! After being kidded about it for several years, and realizing the habit was harming his Christian witness, he broke it. But he also has other habits which he didn't break. For nearly 20 years he has faithfully visited the local jail almost every Sunday afternoon, witnessing to the prisoners about what the Lord can do for them.

Usually he takes some others along, but even if no one is willing to go he is still there. A habit? Yes! But a good one, an inspiring and productive one. Many have come to Christ as a result of this habit.

Habits are the result of repetition of an act. Repetition of whatever we do makes an impression on our minds that can affect us in several ways. It can help us to become more proficient in accomplishing tasks. It can make a task less distasteful since we let our mind go elsewhere when we are doing it. It can develop an unconscious desire to repeat the task whether it is good or bad. It can develop a compulsion that is so strong it is difficult not to follow it.

Habits, thus developed through repetition, can be classified in several degrees that are important for our discussion here. These can be: (1) A regular act that is meaningful, helpful or necessary, (2) A routine act that has become less meaningful, (3) A ritual that has become almost meaningless, (4) An unconscious act that is a "conditioned" reflex or automatic response or reaction, or (5) A compulsive act over which a person has little control.

Much of what we do each day we do from habit. We wake at a certain hour, bathe, shave, dress, eat, travel to work, perform our job, watch television, and read certain newspapers or magazines. Our spiritual life can be developed into a repetitive pattern as well, including Bible reading, Bible study, prayer, witnessing, worship, church attendance, tithing, and visiting.

To allow anything we do to become so ingrained in us that we don't think about it can be dangerous. This can be true even in the good habits we develop. It certainly then is even more true in the bad habits that entangle us.

Without attempting to spell out the good and the bad (you know what's right and what's wrong), let's look at the effect that habits have on us as Christians and how we can use them or avoid them in developing a witness and a testimony to those around us.

Food and drink, for instance, can certainly become a habit. Most of us eat three times each day and some only once (continuously from early morning to late evening). The hours at which we eat and the food we eat are repetitious and very habit-forming, yet this is an essential activity. As someone has said, "Some people eat to live, others live to eat."

Eating can be and should be an enjoyable experience, even though it is as routine as it is. And some become habitual in the amounts they eat as well as the kind of food they eat. In most cases overweight is largely the result of a habit of overeating that has developed a conditioned reflex in our body. This reflex craves food and we call it hunger pangs. It may be totally unrelated to our caloric requirements but because of habit and our biological response we continue to eat more than we burn up in exercise.

The Russian scientist Pavlov, in his famous experiment, proved this concept years ago. He set a metronome going (the ticktock musicians use) for an extended period of time just before feeding a dog each day. The dog became conditioned to the fact that every time he heard the "ticktock" he was going to receive food and his saliva began to flow. After a time the food was withheld but the "ticktock" continued to generate the saliva just the same. Our eating brings a similar response. At mealtime we get hungry and anticipate food whether or not our body needs it, just because of habit. As Christians who provide a place of residence for the Holy Spirit within us, we must be careful to analyze what we are allowing to control our bodies and minds, and the effect that it has on us and others.

In overeating, for example, we can harm ourselves, we can create an unbecoming appearance to others, and we can indulge in an activity that is repulsive to others. Further, we can project the image to those in the world without that we are a gluttonous people. How can any of this help in winning souls for Christ? It can't! And we should exercise care for this reason.

This also can apply to other habits such as the use of tobacco, alcoholic beverages, our recreation and leisure activities, the way we drive our automobile, our personal appearance, our words, our attitudes, and the way we treat people.

In this regard, a Christian should be careful in two important aspects of habits.

1. No action should be so habitual that it becomes an unconscious act or a compulsive act. We should be in control of our actions at all times and should be capable of allowing the Holy Spirit to guide us as well. Even our good habits, our Bible Study, our witnessing and prayer, should be done knowingly and carefully, not as a result of an unconscious or compulsive habit.

2. Actions or appearances that are not becoming or that make the life of a Christian undesirable to others in any way, should be avoided. A Christian's actions, including habits which may be annoying to others, should always be as desirable as possible or

at least as inoffensive as possible if we are to properly represent the Christ we love.

Habits? Yes! But only those becoming to a Christian and which are kept in a controlled and meaningful perspective at all times.

8

God Calls Us From
as Well as To

"The Lord called me to preach," or "The Lord called me to the Philippines." How often have you heard a simple statement like this by those serving the Lord and how often have you been puzzled about how the Lord issues such a call? Or how can you be so sure that it is that kind of permanent call when it comes? This obviously bothers a lot of people, particularly those of us who have not been "called" to preach or go to the mission field. I have no quarrel with those who feel they have been so called. But I would offer a little more careful analysis of how we interpret "the calling" to which so many have strong commitments.

My dad had a problem with this too. When the Lord dealt with him in a series of revival meetings at age 35, he dedicated his life to the Lord anew. "To me, service to the Lord meant the ministry or missionary work," he would tell his audiences. "I couldn't speak correct English in private, let alone stand up before a congregation. But I had done some work for a local mission and I knew from talks with my sisters, Sarah and Marie, who were missionaries to China, that there was much needed work I could do there in that field. But was that what He wanted me to do?

"With this doubt still with me, I went to see my pastor. He listened to my concern. I asked him if he felt God wanted me to serve as a missionary. I had just promised God I would do anything He wanted me to do from that moment. Of course, I explained to the pastor that if I were to go as a missionary it would take some time since I had some debts I would need to pay off first.

"We both knelt in prayer, with each of us asking God for direction. When we arose from our knees my pastor turned to me and said, 'You know God needs businessmen, too.' I looked him in the eye and said, 'All right, I'll be God's businessman,' and that has been my calling ever since."

This illustrates several points about the Christian "calling."

1. Our calling does not necessarily need to be to a particular profession or location. Most references to calling in the Scripture are aimed at a total dedication of our lives to Christ Jesus wherever He will lead us after that point. "That ye would walk worthy of God, who hath called you unto His kingdom and glory" (1 Thes. 2:12). Dad did this when he accepted the challenge in the revival meeting and dedicated his life to Christ, not knowing where this might lead. He was quite willing to sell the machinery he loved and go as a missionary if that was the Lord's will. The important thing here is that we must be totally sold out to the Lord or totally committed, regardless of where the Lord leads. In other words, we must first be willing to go

anywhere or do anything before God will show us the next step. This is a lifetime commitment, not just when things are going good, or not just for a few years until we change our mind. If it is not for a lifetime then you haven't made the commitment. If you haven't met this requirement then the other concepts of calling do not even apply to you.

2. There is a different kind of call to a specific location, a specific act, or a specific vocation. This is different from the first type and is best illustrated by Paul in Ephesians. "I, therefore . . . beseech you that ye walk worthy of the vocation wherewith ye are called" (Eph. 4:1). This verse really relates more to guidance than to a calling, but since the term "calling" is so widely used in this context, I have included it here. The main difference is not in the level of dedication or commitment, for this should be as great or nearly as great as the basic commitment above. The difference lies solely in the time element involved. The first is for a lifetime— all or none. This second one is for varying lengths of time, *as God chooses*.

A call may be for a lifetime or may eventually become for a lifetime. When this occurs, however, it is only because God did not choose to give new direction, and *not* because this calling was irrevocable. This is where I believe many of God's servants misinterpret this matter of calling.

To say, "God has called me to preach and for that reason I can never do anything else" as some do, creates problems for me. It sounds as if they heard God one time and then "turned Him off" on that particular subject. I just can't buy that. I firmly believe that God even calls preachers and missionaries out of that so-called high calling (more on that later) into other more mundane vocations when such is for His own purpose and grace (more on this too).

In my early years in college administration this question regarding a call was brought home forcefully to me in dealing with a pastor whom we engaged as a chaplain for the college. He functioned well in chapel services and in general ministries, but when I suggested that it would be beneficial to the students for him to become involved in a broader scope of activities including teaching and counseling he refused.

He informed me that not only had God called him to preach, and this was a lifetime commitment for him, but that preaching was the highest calling there was and God *never* calls anyone to a lower calling after once calling him to preach. If this were true and if all preachers believed this way, the teachers in our seminary who teach our preachers could never teach from experience because a preacher could never step "down" from this calling in order to teach. Sounds ridiculous doesn't it? It is. Each of us must make our commitment to God and then permit God to lead us, using good sense in our perception of His leading in each period of life.

While Dad perceived God's calling to him at that moment to be God's businessman, he nevertheless, over the remainder of his life "preached" more messages than a great many pastors, and had a greater impact on mission fields than most missionaries.

Even Paul, who was probably the greatest preacher of all times, was really a lay preacher who worked in a profession for much of his income. God does not call us into a narrow channel of service that never changes. He calls us to service that may be broad or narrow, may be straight or widely varied according to His good pleasure, and we had better be listening when He expresses His pleasure to us.

3. The Scripture talks about a high calling, "I press toward the mark for the prize of the high calling of God in Christ Jesus" (Phil. 3:14).

In another place Paul called it a "holy calling": "Who hath saved us and called us with an holy calling, not according to our works, but according to His own purpose and grace, which was given in Christ Jesus before the world began" (2 Tim. 1:9).

Some assume that there is a special vocation or activity that is God's high or highest calling. This may be true, but allow me to qualify this a little further. First, I believe the high calling refers to our basic commitment to Christ—to the whatever, whenever, "I'm willing" part of it. Second, I believe that to whatever and wherever God leads us as *individuals* is God's high and holy calling to us— but for us alone. For someone else it may be different. There is no vocation, direction, or location that is classified as the high or highest calling for everyone. God's highest calling for you is the place where He wants *you*. His highest calling for someone else is the place where He wants them. If we are totally committed to Christ and have been open to guidance, we are in His highest calling regardless of what we are doing. And this calling may change from year to year.

God first called me into the business world and into the management of Dad's company. I *know* that. Then later He called me from that into the educational world and into college administration for nearly ten years. I *know* that. But then the call was just as specific back into corporate management again for a period of six years when Dad was forced to retire. Now, I'm back in educational administration again. God didn't change His mind. I didn't change my mind. This was all part of His detailed plan and His guidance which I was attempting to follow; each time I'm firmly convinced that I was in His highest calling because that was where He wanted *me*.

4. Our calling is for God's purpose and plan, not for our own (2 Tim. 1:9). If you set goals for your life—if you develop targets at which you are shooting, and I agree with this concept, be sure you include the Lord in the development of these goals and targets so that He isn't forced to change them for you. Also, remember that goals are just goals and there may be occasions when God's plan is to sidetrack you from them. We must be willing to accept that sidetrack without it affecting our ability to persevere toward that or other goals. But God really gives us a great deal of latitude, normally. As long as we are really willing to go anywhere or do anything, we will quite often find that He will allow us to do just what we wanted to do in the first place. If not, He will change our wants so that we are quite happy and satisfied in the direction He leads us.

In seeking God's calling for you specifically, remember the first call you must answer is to total surrender to His will. Until you do that, the other calls you may "hear" or think you hear really don't count. Beyond that, God's call for you will be His highest calling, but be sure to keep your eyes, ears, mind, and heart open in the future, because God's call is like a road map which you must continually refer to in order to make the proper turns and stay on the right highway through life's journey.

If you are planning an auto trip from say, Parkersburg, West Virginia to Billings, Montana, you wouldn't get into just any old parked car on the street and then start looking for "Billings, Montana" signs. First, you would have, or obtain, a car of your own that was capable of getting you there. This is the preparation part that is necessary before God can take us through life.

Then you would get some road maps that would show you what highway to turn onto and the general directions to head. God doesn't often give us an entire map of our lives (it would scare some of us to death if He did), but He gives us all we need to have. His road map, of course, is His Holy Word. Then at each junction in the road we will find signs that will point us in the right direction and to the right highway if we (1) look at the right part of the map, and, (2) have been following it closely enough to know where we are.

Similarly at each juncture in life, God will give us signposts to point the direction *if* we have been following His leading closely enough to know where we are and if we will look in His Word for our current instructions.

God's directional calling for us is the road map He has developed for our life and which He will reveal to us step-by-step as we meet the conditions and requirements set forth for us.

9

Never Give Up! Unless, of Course, God Says So

One of the seeming conflicts that troubles a great many Christians is in knowing when to stay in there fighting for a principle or for success, and when to accept the situation or station in life that God has put us in without pressing to get out of it. This centers around the conflict between what I will call "perseverance" and "acceptance."

Both are sound and solid spiritual concepts and Paul addresses both of them. "And let us not be weary in well-doing; for in due season we shall reap, if we faint not" (Gal. 6:9). In another place Paul wrote: "Why not just accept mistreatment and leave it at that?" (1 Cor. 6:7, LB)

While each of these two topics could create a complete discussion in itself, they dare not be separated for our discussion here, for they really are inseparable. It is a paradox that we are cautioned and challenged in the Scriptures to accept whatever befalls us, yet at the same time to persevere and not be weary in well-doing. How can these be reconciled? This is one of the exciting facets of our spiritual lives. God, through His Holy Spirit, can give us the wisdom to differentiate between these two, along with the grace to accept and the strength to persevere. Let's look at each separately and get a better feel for how they relate to us.

Acceptance

Scripture is very clear on this matter of accepting or receiving with satisfaction the station in life, the calling in life, and the activity to which God has called us. Sometimes these aren't always to our liking but God will give us the grace to accept whatever they may be without bitterness, without recrimination, and without looking back. These difficult situations can be a delayed answer to prayer, they can be situations within which we must work, that are controlled by others, that we are not able to change, or it may be that God is just telling us to back off and accept whatever it may be in our lives. Extreme caution must be exercised in acceptance, however, that we do not develop a "martyr complex," taking pride (which is unscriptural) in the martyrdom to which we have been called and thus destroying our ability to persevere when the situation requires it.

In my father's career as a successful Christian businessman, he faced many of these situations. On several occasions he would design and build a new construction machine that even after many trials just would not work or would not do the job. He would persevere up to a point, and perseverance was really one of his specialties. Then he would make a decision to abandon the idea. The machine would be scrapped and he would go on about his business never looking back.

This philosophy applied not only to machines but to enterprises. For 14 years we operated an industrial missionary project in Liberia, West Africa, a project into which he had put millions of dollars and a significant part of his life's energy. When I explained to him one day the most recent developments and how it appeared unwise to continue the project, he very matter-of-factly said, "Okay, let's close it down." Without any trauma, recrimination or sulking, he immediately went back to his drawing board to work on a new machine on which he was pressing forward at the moment.

After Dad's homegoing in 1969, and the merger of the corporation into another firm a year or so later, I found myself in an enviable position as a senior vice-president of a large corporation with a personal income approaching $100,000 per year. After a couple of years in this situation I began to realize that this was not really where the Lord wanted me and was not where I could be of most service to Him. Without having any idea what I would do, I accepted this as from the Lord and walked away from that job, leaving behind not only the salary but also giving up a majority of my savings on a stock-option purchase which I could not control. Since that time I have earned only a fraction of that salary. But I have accepted the place the Lord has put me and the way in which He is permitting me to witness for Him through LeTourneau College. I have absolutely no regrets in following the Lord's will.

The primary caution which must be exercised in this teaching about acceptance is that, aside from very specific direction from the Lord, or involvement in things which are not scriptural, we are commanded to run with patience the race that is set before us. We are told to persevere as long as we can continue to progress and to change the circumstances in which we find ourselves. It is only when God specially directs or when the control is totally out of our hands that we must exercise acceptance.

Perseverance

Just as faith must also include works, acceptance must also include perseverance, in order to accomplish things beyond what we have done or think we can do. We must not persevere, however, to the point that we cannot discern when the acceptance of an alternative is necessary in God's plan. Most Christians give up too soon, however, under the pretext that if God wants it done, He'll do it somehow, through someone, and we shouldn't run ahead of Him. There are cases where this may be true, but my observation and experience indicate that we usually don't follow through sufficiently. Many times we are just not willing to put forth that extra effort from the strength and wisdom God will make available to us to get the job done. Remember, God is still omnipotent and if He thinks we have pushed too far He is certainly capable of shutting doors completely in front of us so that it is literally impossible for us to go further.

Dad faced bankruptcy several times in his business career. Each time when a lawyer or a business associate would attempt to persuade him to accept voluntary bankruptcy he would literally laugh in their faces and show them the door. He refused to accept such an alternative because he felt it would be dishonoring to the Lord, and because he felt he should continue to persevere himself to correct whatever situation had developed causing that condition. Each time he was right and the business recovered handsomely.

In his designing of heavy machinery he didn't always discard a machine that didn't work either. On many occasions he remodeled and redesigned machines dozens of times, eventually correcting problems and making them work as they were originally intended. This perseverance was really one of his secrets of success. He never gave up on anything until the Lord appeared to have shut the door tightly on him. He would never accept a closed door when he perceived it to be a human action or personal failure, but consistently pressed forward to do things others considered impossible. He staunchly believed that we are intended to be "more than conquerors through Him" (Rom. 8:37), and he was determined to fill that role. Yet he had that strange and quiet inner sensitivity to God so that on those rare and special occasions, as I have mentioned, he quietly and quickly backed off and never looked back with regret.

As Christians we should be challenged to develop the grace to accept, the strength to persevere, and the wisdom to know the difference.

10

The Twin Scourges of Society

"If God intended for us to smoke tobacco, He would have put a chimney in our head."

"What's wrong with wine? Jesus, Himself, turned water into wine for a wedding feast."

Have you ever heard statements like these before? Of course, you have. Many well-intentioned Christians miss the point completely when they deal with these two issues. And in doing so they probably do more harm than good in getting the real problem across to our young people, who say we are already too negative.

The use of tobacco and alcohol in society today and its relationship to Christianity, as well as to ethical and legal conduct, is greatly misunderstood by devout Christians, liberal Christians, and non-Christians. I know I'm in trouble with you on this one already for attempting to classify Christians into two groups, but bear with me and hear me out and I'll try not to "blow it up" too big in an effort to get you to "see it better."

Tobacco

Tobacco has long enveloped society as a habit that, while certainly not pleasant in terms of cleanliness, nor beneficial to anyone, has become an almost uncontrollable force in our society. Its devastating effects on the human lungs have been proven without question; yet it continues nearly unabated as a national pastime. Even eliminating its use in most public places has still not diminished its sales or its effect. But, as bad as this is, the use of tobacco is not a sin and is not forbidden in God's Word.

Yes, I know! You immediately bring up the point that our body is the temple of the Holy Spirit (which it is) and that we shouldn't defile our body (which we shouldn't). And I agree that this is reason enough to avoid the use of tobacco. But if you hang all of your reasoning on that fact alone, you are in trouble. Why? Because there are other things we do that are just as harmful to our bodies. Overeating, for instance! Oops! Now I've gone into meddling! But I've talked about that elsewhere in this book. At this point, let me just say that tobacco is wrong for several reasons, including the one just cited. But let's look in this chapter at a more practical or defensible way to classify it in the life of a Christian.

Alcohol

While wine and strong drink were forbidden of priests by law in the Old Testament (Lev. 10:9), drinking apparently was an accepted practice in New Testament Christianity—up to a point. If we use the Old Testament Law to prohibit strong drink, which many do, we must be extremely careful because there are many other facets of the Law that we don't and can't observe. To observe part of it without all of it is "righteousness" which Scripture tells us is "filthy rags" (Isa. 64:6). Therefore, since we are under grace we must assume that strong drink is not really forbidden to the Christian—nor is it a sin as many seem to claim, but like tobacco, it is still wrong for another reason. Let me explain.

Other than those things which are clearly defined as sin in New Testament Christianity under grace, there are many things which Christians should avoid for reasons other than sin. They may not be sins but it is extremely important, nevertheless, that we recognize and avoid them. Besides what I would call spiritual absolutes, for which there can be no compromise, these other things come under a classification which I will call Christian cultural standards. These are classified three ways in my book, *Keeping Your Cool in a World of Tension.*

1. Those things which are very difficult to control sufficiently so that they do not *become* spiritual absolutes when they are present in excess or so that they do not *lead* to spiritual absolutes.

2. Those things which make it very difficult to keep our attention focused on spiritual things when these are present.

3. Those things which are so inconsistent in the minds of others outside of Christianity with what *they* believe a Christian should be that it is difficult for them to see the values and the Gospel which we represent and become a stumbling block.

When we place tobacco under this scrutiny, we find that the discourteous conduct which it encourages in causing others to breathe the smoke, and the image with which it has been associated, put it in the category of a negative for a Christian. It is certainly a stumbling block, and its habit-forming character may create other conflicts with your testimony as well.

When we place strong drink under this scrutiny, we find that normally it can be eliminated by the first two, depending on to what extent and in what culture it is practiced, but when viewed in the third category it certainly *must* be eliminated. Not because it is a sin, but because it is definitely a stumbling block. "It is good neither to eat flesh, nor to drink wine, nor anything whereby thy brother stumbleth or is offended, or is made weak" (Rom. 14:21).

For these reasons, we do not permit the use of tobacco at LeTourneau College. We also have a rule that results in automatic expulsion of a student if he becomes involved with intoxicating beverages in any way. We have this rule for two reasons. First, we are a training ground for young people and we feel that they should be impressed early in life with the dangers of alcohol and the importance of abstinence from both a heartache and a testimony standpoint.

Second, each student is a part of what becomes LeTourneau College to the various publics around us and they are part of the testimony and image of the college as well as being their own testimony and image. As administrators charged by the Lord with not allowing the college itself, in a broad sense, to become a stumbling block, we must protect the college's testimony with a strict enforcement of this particular rule.

Let me hasten to add that strong drink *is* a sin when it is used excessively and affects our ability to think and act clearly and rationally, and it is this side of it that causes all the pain, heartache, suffering, and death we see.

But, because it really can't be adequately controlled by Christians, or non-Christians, either, I personally feel it should be eliminated from society, and tobacco as well.

What makes it difficult to get this point across to young people, however, is that we as adults are hypocrites in the way we approach this and many other values that we place on our long list of negatives for the younger generation.

First, we misclassify what our objections to tobacco and alcohol really are. They are Christian cultural standards that are extremely important to observe, but in themselves they are not sin. Then we gloss over very lightly in our own lives, and fail miserably to observe, some very specific spiritual absolutes which *are* sin, such as pride, lying, gossip, deceit, and dishonesty. It's no wonder the young people are confused when we hypocritically indulge in sin ourselves and then try to classify as sin things that really aren't.

Devout Christians may classify tobacco and strong drink as sin, which they aren't. Liberal Christians may indulge in them, which they shouldn't. And non-Christians may fail to recognize the hazards involved and the blight on our society that they represent completely apart from Christianity.

Tobacco or alcohol in any form? No! But then, let's not be pious about it by misrepresenting it, nor hypocritical about it by indulging in other practices which are really forbidden by God's Word.

Part V Five Misunderstandings

11

Do You Really Want God's Guidance?

Have you ever heard a speaker start out a message with something like this? "If someone had told me two years ago that I would be doing what I'm doing today, I would have told him he was crazy."

I have heard it—from missionaries, teachers, pastors, and others.

A missionary friend who was very productive in an African field, and had just moved into service as director of a Bible school for nationals, had such an experience. He was at what might have been termed his peak of service, yet the Lord (through his superiors) called him back to the U.S. for administrative service. He felt out of place, yet responded to what he felt was God's will for him and submitted to the authority of those with whom he was serving. The result? His knowledge and real concern for what was happening in the field made him extremely effective in his administrative position. He was actually able to multiply himself several times through others sent to the field.

Many professional men, such as doctors, dentists, engineers, and others, have been led, through a series of events, out of their routine secular job into short or long term service on the mission field. Their real value on the field was because they had such thorough training and experience in their profession. If God had called them to the mission field to begin with they probably would never have received this training and experience.

So God works in mysterious ways, His wonders to perform. He leads us sometimes through professions, jobs, experiences, and even great testings, just so we'll be properly prepared for the job He has for us to do somewhere, sometime. We can *never* feel that we have fully arrived at the place where God wants us, and that we'll just stay there and work for Him the rest of our lives. We must always be sensitive to God's will and His guidance.

I have had many such experiences, myself. Responding to God's leading through my dad, I prepared for and accepted responsibilities in manufacturing and industry. Since Dad had little respect for the type of colleges he saw in operation in those days, I even by-passed a college education in order to learn the more practical side of the business from the ground up. So where did I end up? After nearly twenty years on the practical firing line, God sent me back to school to get the proper theoretical degrees and then made me a college president. But since God wanted a different kind of college and needed a different kind of president to be responsible for it, He had to route me through another profession first to make sure I knew what business, industry, and engineering were really all about before He could trust me in that job. Then, too, I needed maturity and growth as well, and this was God's chosen way of giving me some "basic training."

Have I now arrived at the ultimate—where God wants me? Absolutely not! While God may be making me productive where I am, I have no assurance that this is not also a training ground for yet another field of service. God made me productive in industry, also, but even that was part of my training. He is constantly able to use us wherever we are and, even though He has other things in mind for us eventually, He'll make us useful to Him where we are.

Even retirement is no indication that we are to conclude our training and our service. My dad didn't even start the industrial missionary projects in Liberia and Peru until he was 65 years of age. And from the enthusiasm and hard work he put into it, you'd have thought he was planning to go on for another 25 years. He almost did, too!

Another close friend of mine was a pastor and church administrator in this country all his life until his retirement. Then God led him into overseas evangelism. He will tell you today after seven years that he has led more people to Christ since he retired than in his entire life before that. And he's still going strong. He was an active soul-winner in his previous ministry, too.

But how do we know when God is leading us? How can we be sure when an opportunity for a change in direction comes along? These questions seem to bother many sincere Christians today. I can't answer them specifically for you, but I believe that it is possible for God to work through your own mind and reason. A simple procedure will allow God to coordinate your mind with the circumstances around you so that you can move ahead with peace and confidence concerning the future and how God is guiding you.

Our military missiles of the late 20th century will illustrate. These missiles have what we call "guidance" systems built into them. Some missiles respond to instruction signals given to them from a source miles away. Others depend entirely on a target, at which they are aimed, to control their "steering" mechanism and to keep them on track. Certain missiles have a photo response; after being locked in on a spot on the scene they are looking at, they can "remember" that particular spot and guide themselves to it.

If God can create a complex world that operates on such a precise system of laws and science that man has been able to predetermine and predict precisely what can and will happen—don't you think this same God is also able to transmit signals to the mind He has created within you so that you can know His will and direction? "And thine ears shall hear a word behind thee, saying, 'This is the way, walk ye in it,' when ye turn to the right hand, and when ye turn to the left" (Isa. 30:21).

We Christians like to talk in clichés. The phenomenon I am talking about is the "still small voice" that we have heard many talk about. Did they actually hear an audible voice? Probably not, although it is certainly possible! More likely, their mind was responding to something God was communicating to them and this was just a more rational way of explaining what happened.

Look at a simpler system than the guided missile. We're all very familiar with the radio in our home, our car, or even in our pocket!

The place where you are now located and the air around you is literally jam-packed with all kinds of radio signals—thousands of them. There is not anywhere on the face of this earth where this would not be true today. We're not actually aware of it. We're certainly not conscious of it. Why? Because we don't have the precision instruments, or devices to transform radio frequency waves into sound waves.

There could be a weather warning or tornado approaching you this very minute and you wouldn't know it. Your local radio and television stations could be shouting "take for cover" warnings continuously, but you wouldn't know it if you didn't have the facilities to listen to those warnings. Radio signals are everywhere around us. Yet, unless we have the electronic devices to convert them into sound waves that our ears can hear, we might have difficulty believing that they really are present.

God's communication to us is similarly everywhere around us. But unless we have the proper relationship and attitudes toward God (the equipment) we may have difficulty believing that such communication actually exists.

How do we get this "equipment" with which to receive these spiritual signals? It has to be developed over a period of years through experience, heartaches, trust, victories, study, and communication with God through prayer. Radios haven't always been as sensitive and as able to distinguish one signal from another as they are today. It took years of experience, development, testing, production, and use to be able to build a radio that can be sufficiently selective to reject a 500,000-watt station a few blocks away and yet still be able to tune in clearly a 10-watt station that is halfway around the world. I've done just that with an amateur radio receiver.

It's not easy. The set is complicated and it took years of development to get it to that degree of selectivity. But if God can create the laws behind their use and then show man how to discover and use those laws, He can also help us to develop the sensitivity and selectivity that is necessary to use them. We can tune out or reject the loud and blatant signals Satan is throwing at us from all sides, in order to tune in on that particular signal that God has for us at that special time when we need it.

What's the procedure for tuning in this signal from God? It's not so much a procedure as it is a condition. We must have the right circuits built into our lives. These are in the form of a relationship and attitude toward God. God can't talk to us if we're not on speaking terms with Him.

First, we must be born again. A dead person can't hear someone talk to him. If we're dead spiritually, we can't expect to hear spiritual communication. Then we must walk closely with God. Talking to Him and listening to Him (reading His Word) daily. James wrote:

If you want to know what God wants you to do, ask Him, and He will gladly tell you, for He is always ready to give a bountiful supply of wisdom to all who ask Him; He will not resent it. But when you ask Him, be sure that you really expect Him to tell you, for a doubtful mind will be as unsettled as a wave of the sea that is driven and tossed by the wind; and every decision you then make will be uncertain, as you turn first this way, and then that. If you don't ask with faith, don't expect the Lord to give you any solid answer (James 1:5-8, LB).

If you can honestly meet the conditions above as well as these set forth by James, you should have no problem. It's just that simple. When you have built these conditions and attitudes into your life then you may accept the circumstances around you as God's leading, or you may do what seems best if there are choices to make. As long as you don't try to do something forbidden by God's Word, you can accept what makes the most sense to you at the moment. If you make a wrong move and you have really met these conditions, God will close the door so you won't make the wrong choice. There will be no doubt in your mind when it happens. Otherwise, you can be sure that He will communicate with your mind so that your choice will be His choice.

One of the most helpful comments on this subject of guidance that I have seen was written by the late A. W. Tozer. It is a tract titled, "How The Lord Leads," and is available from Christian Publications.

God has promised to guide us. He will guide us. He is anxious to guide us. But we were created with a free will, and God will not force this guidance on us. We must build a relationship with God so that He knows we want His guidance and will follow it. With such a built-in guidance system in our lives, we will be able to respond to each minute signal from God and keep our life course and daily decisions constantly adjusted to the plan and fulfillment He has for us.

12

Thou Shalt Not . . . Thou Shalt Not . . . Thou Shalt Not!

Great misunderstanding seems to surround the many negatives or don'ts that have become such a part of our lives. While this is a critical area for all of us, the problem becomes most visible to us in relationship to our youth.

A great misunderstanding has evolved in the minds of many of today's teenage and college-age youth about the negatives on which the older generation harps so much. A similar misunderstanding is present in defining the freedoms young people desire so strongly. In another chapter we deal with the matter of freedom but let's now examine the subject of negatives and how they relate to these freedoms.

American society has become extremely complex with many varied and complex personal interrelationships and values. And this complexity has also increased greatly in the past twenty years, more than most of us in the older generation are willing to recognize.

Because we live in a basically free society, we should dwell largely on positive values and behavioral patterns rather than negative ones, but we don't. Over the years we have developed a whole system of negatives that are important and necessary to support our freedoms. Both the negatives and the freedoms are necessary and complimentary. We break down in our communication between generations in two basic ways.

First, we, the older generation, tend to gather all of our negatives together in a neat little package and expect to sell this package to our young people without classification or stratification. We expect young people to "take our word" that these negatives are wrong and that our experience has shown them to be improper.

If they had proper respect for us, they really should accept our judgment in this. But then we "blow" the whole thing by living such hypocritical lives ourselves in relationship to our neat little package of negatives that we have created for them. We shouldn't be surprised when intelligent young people see through the sham. We forget that while we may have "accepted" this value system without question from our parents and elders when we were younger, our young people today are smarter and much more educated than we were at the same age, and, for that reason, easily see through our hypocrisy.

Second, some of the younger generation have also insisted on wrapping up their desires for freedoms in a neat little package, demanding them from society without the definitions and responsibilities which these freedoms entail. Their hypocrisy also shows through when the freedoms which they demand actually deny freedoms to so many others who also have rights. For you to have freedom to do a particular thing means that everyone else around you is restricted from doing anything that will interfere with your freedom. On the other hand, for others to have their freedoms means that you are restricted from anything which might interfere with their freedom. For example, how can the question of freedom be resolved when two people are thrown together in a poorly ventilated public place, one person with the "right" to smoke tobacco and the other with the "right" to breathe unpolluted air? Obviously the rights of freedoms of one of them must be restricted. This example of smoking is a very common problem and even the airlines and restaurants have not found a really satisfactory solution.

You can readily see that questions of negatives or restrictions and of freedoms or rights are certainly not simple ones. Nor are the problems easily defined or communicated so that all can understand. With so many people living together in the world, with daily interrelationships with each other, even the secular society has had to develop a very complex system of behavioral codes, both legal and implied.

The legal codes are the laws that have been developed for the protection of life and property and for the preservation of order. To kill or to injure a person takes away his freedoms, so we have made laws against killing and injuring.

We have also adopted implied codes in our society based on common courtesy and, while they are not laws carrying legal penalties, they may carry social penalties. We are taught to knock on doors before entering as a courtesy to preserve another person's right or freedom of privacy. We use the terms "please" and "thank you" when we ask someone else to do something for us that might reduce their freedoms while allowing us to exercise ours more.

Because of these complex interrelations with people, not all behavioral codes that we adopt, whether legal or implied, seem to be fair to everyone. In fact, many of them will definitely favor the freedoms of some people while placing heavy negatives on others. And because these laws and codes are developed by people who may err, their biases frequently make them unjust. Nevertheless, they must exist, or confusion and chaos would reign. Many of these seem arbitrary. For example, why remain stopped at a red traffic light when there are no other cars within blocks of you?

Many of the freedoms the younger generation demands appear to be arbitrary and unnecessary to us, and likewise, many of our negatives appear to be arbitrary and unnecessary to them.

The ability to communicate the need for both the "legal" negatives, for survival and protection, and the "courtesy" negatives, for harmonious relationships, seems to have broken down. We have also failed to communicate the responsibility and the personal integrity involved in the freedoms which our young people demand.

Even from a secular viewpoint this inability can be a real problem. Riots and civil disorder have become commonplace in recent years among some of our youth. With Christian behavior patterns, however, the situation can get even more complex, and we need even more of the right kind of communication because of the extra negatives which the Christian home and Christian society have adopted.

In Christianity we have added additional codes beyond the legal code and the courtesy code we have just mentioned. These overlap considerably with the first two, but they also vary in some important aspects. For Christians there is the spiritual code which is set forth in the Bible, and which I have chosen to call "spiritual absolutes." This code of behavior includes those things which are specifically commanded or forbidden by the Word of God and which if not followed are, in themselves, "sin."

Then, in addition to these spiritual absolutes, there is also a code of cultural behavior that has been adopted by late 20th century Christians in America. This code may not have been as important in other periods of time and may not even now be as important in other countries or areas of the world. In fact, this code may vary considerably even within our own various denominations, groups, and sections of our own country. These additional codes may not be spiritual absolutes, but they, nevertheless, constitute an important behavioral pattern for us to communicate to the younger generation. These must be communicated, however, for what they really are. These codes, beyond the spiritual absolutes, fall into the three basic classifications of "Christian Cultural Standards" already mentioned in the chapter on tobacco and alcohol, but are repeated to refresh your memory.

1. Those things which are so difficult to control that they may become spiritual absolutes when they are present in excess, or so that they do lead to spiritual absolutes. Excess of almost anything might fall into this category.

2. Those things which, when present, make it very difficult for us to keep our attention focused on spiritual things. Even sports might be a problem to some people here.

3. Those things which are so inconsistent in the minds of others outside of Christianity with what they believe a Christian should be, that it is difficult for them to see the values and the Gospel which we represent, and we become a "stumbling block." (This includes a whole gamut of things which the world considers are inconsistent with the image of Christianity).

Many of the negatives of Christian living fall into one of these three categories rather than being a spiritual absolute. These negatives may still be wrong for a Christian to practice but, because the older generation attempts to classify these Christian cultural standards as sin or as spiritual absolutes, many young people reject the inclusion of them in our neat little package of spiritual rules.

As mentioned earlier our communication to Christian youth breaks down in two ways:

First, we categorize all Christian negatives as sin or spiritual absolutes and expect our youth to accept the package without question.

We need to admit the differences between the spiritual absolutes of the Scripture and the Christian cultural standards that we have added to them. I have enough faith in our young people to believe they will then be more willing to understand and observe all of them. Christian cultural standards must be subject to change with the times, our circumstances and society around us.

Second, we adults have ignored some very vital spiritual absolutes ourselves, creating a hypocrisy that complicates even more the communication and the importance of Christian cultural standards for our youth. For some reason we consider the spiritual absolutes, sins of the mind and tongue, to be less important than those of the hand or body. Certainly sin is sin. Pride, lying, gossip, deceit, and dishonestly, to name a few, are just as much spiritual absolutes as are adultery, murder, and stealing. But when we wink at gossip, which is a real sin, how can we expect to convince our young men that long hair may be wrong when that is really not a sin but only a cultural practice, which may be important to Christians today but not tomorrow or in another setting? Whether we permit or condemn this or any other Christian cultural practice is a matter of individual conviction and conscience; we must be certain to get our priorities and definitions straight between sin and cultural practices before we begin making an issue of them.

If we, as mature experienced adults, could ever get our own thinking and practice straight on (1) the classification of these negatives, and (2) our hypocrisy in dealing with real sin, then we might be better able to explain, justify, and convince our young people of the importance of even the Christian cultural standards which we espouse so highly.

I would urge anyone dealing with young people to make a personal search of the Scriptures and see for himself how few of what are considered to be important negatives really are spiritual absolutes and also how many of the spiritual absolutes he may be ignoring himself. This could be shocking. But it does make it possible to be more understanding, more capable of explaining the necessity of the cultural standards, and more consistent in your own Christian experience.

13

Climbing the Ladder

Ask anyone, particularly those under 40, if they would like to continue in the job or at the level they are now at for the rest of their lives. The answer will probably be "No!" Most of us want to continue to improve ourselves and to rise to something better or more important than what we are now doing. The problem is that few of those who want to advance in their job or profession are really willing to spend the time and effort necessary to prepare properly for such an advancement.

Living today is much more complex than when our country was founded 200 years ago. There may have been a time then when a person could be a generalist and learn to provide all the basic necessities for his living, not worrying about interaction with other people. This is not true today. Our society is so complex that each of us must be a specialist in one way or another. Even the farmer today can no longer farm in the simple ways of years gone by. He, too, is very much a specialist.

For this reason it becomes necessary that each of us become prepared for whatever specialist role

we can or will perform in society. The machinist
who aspires to be a department foreman may need
to learn something about product costs, human relations, and areas which he may not have known
even existed before his advancement. We have
many young people who come to college wanting
to learn engineering because they like automotive
mechanics and have worked on their own automobiles. Yet they are unwilling to take the time to
learn English, math, and other courses that are a
required and necessary part of an engineering cur-
riculum. They feel these courses are unnecessary
for what they want to do in life. Yet an engineer
who cannot properly use the English language to
communicate with his superiors, in reports or in the
explanation of a machine, can't go very far as an
engineer.

One of the big problems that we had in colleges
during the '60s was that it became the "in" thing
to get a college education in the new space age.
(Avoiding the draft helped swell the ranks of
college students, also). In this situation, however,
there were many students who had no real purpose
for being there other than that it was the thing to
do. With no purpose or commitment they began
to look for causes to champion and unhealthy activities to fill this void. The 70s seemed to have
brought something of a reversal in this trend. The
draft is over and now there is a great deal of stress
on that fact that a college education is not necessary for everyone and many are taking other avenues of preparation. With this the campus unrest
has subsided greatly. The great majority of students
in college now are there for a purpose or a reason—
not just because it is the thing to do.

Christians have a responsibility and an opportunity in this regard that is not available to others. We can have a purpose or objective and at the same time have the wherewithal to reach it if we will take advantage of the power, strength, and wisdom available to us.

Several years ago I was impressed and encouraged by some comments of a nationally-known evangelical leader who was ministering on our college campus. Not having a naturally outgoing personality myself, I was somewhat reticent in taking certain speaking engagements, particularly to secular groups such as local civic clubs. He set me straight, and I've never forgotten it. He reasoned, "A Christian shouldn't have to take a back seat to anybody. We've got something to talk about that the non-Christian doesn't have, and we've got the total resources of the Holy Spirit to help us get it out." He went on to say, "I never hesitate to talk to *any* group regardless of how frightening they might be to the average person."

Of course, he didn't presume on God by just getting up before such a group and starting to ramble on, expecting God to give him something to say at that moment. Instead, he prepared carefully and thoroughly.

What he meant was that as Christians we have vast resources available to us in what we can talk about, our capabilities to understand and absorb it, and the ability to deliver it. For this reason we ought to be able to do better than anyone else who has to do all this on his own without the help of the Holy Spirit. But we still need to prepare. We just are better *able* to prepare.

Certain things bear careful analysis, however, particularly for the Christian in preparing for an occupation. Some of the major factors, which must be recognized and must be included in the concept and philosophy of preparation, cover a very broad field of occupations and can nearly be universally applied.

There are seven basic necessities that I have identified which any person must have in order to properly equip himself for a particular occupation. I am applying them here in areas with which I am more familiar, but these same seven characteristics are necessary in almost any occupation to which you might aspire that demands leadership, administration, management, or just improving some particular skills within that occupation.

My own particular field of study is business and industry. In teaching an Industrial Management course recently in our college, I developed these seven ideas to convey to my students. These are areas of capability in which a manager or a person aspiring to a management position must excel:

1. *Motivation and Drive.* This has been one of my own weaknesses, so I put it at the head of the list. If you are basically an introvert, shy or retiring, as I am, you may have difficulty with this. It is essential, nevertheless, and because I have allowed God to work in my life, He has given me enough of what I call "manufactured extroversion" (outgoing, comfortable with strangers) to allow me to operate reasonably effectively. A balance must be maintained between, on the one hand, such characteristics as perserverance, works of salesmanship, and on the other hand, acceptance, faith, time for the family, for the Lord, and for recreation. Too much effort or time on one side, at the expense of time or effort on the other side, creates an unbalance, leading to ineffectiveness.

2. *Working with People.* Almost everything we

do in life, we do in cooperation with other people, whether we are a manager or not. The ability to work harmoniously with others in accomplishing a job is one of the important criteria of effectiveness in a manager. A balance must be maintained between, on the one hand, toughness, getting the job done, convictions, and allowing free enterprise to operate and, on the other hand, understanding, ability to relate to people, social reform, and appreciation. In attempting to maintain a balance between some of these extremes, it is important that we are fair, that we admit our own mistakes, that we keep our promises, and that we operate with reasonable consistency. My natural tendency is to be understanding rather than tough. However, I have faced many occasions in business where it was absolutely necessary, in order to get the job done, to be tough and demanding on those with whom I work. But even on those occasions I would make every effort to be fair and consistent in my demands.

3. *Financial Comprehension.* Many people seem to feel that dealing with finances can be left to others. While obviously there are specialists in finance, our economy and systems for living have become so complex that each of us must understand finances to some degree in order to function effectively in almost any vocation. Income taxes, Social Security, insurance, and finance company borrowing have forced all of us to develop some degree of comprehension of money and finance. To ignore this area is to become not very well-rounded in dealing with the world around us. Even pastors and housewives must face the rigors of understanding some of these complex situations. In the business arena the matter of balance in this area comes be-

tween, on the one hand, tight controls and cost responsibility and, on the other hand, dynamics of management and the avoidance of senseless accounting for the inconsequential. Any business organization that puts undue emphasis on one side at the expense of emphasis of the other, cannot long survive in our society.

4. *Communication.* Because we must all work with others in the accomplishment of any of our objectives, whether they be personal, organizational, or spiritual, it becomes of paramount importance that we learn how to communicate with other people so that they understand our needs and values and we understand also their needs and values. Balance is necessary in this area also. On the one hand is written material, which can have greater clarity, can be reread, and which can contain technical and legal information. On the other hand, verbal communication can carry more meaning and inflection, can be more quickly carried out, is less costly, and can build better relationships. Both types of communication are necessary, depending on the individuals and the circumstances, but an effective manager will learn to use both with great discernment rather than using one or the other exclusively.

A recent seminar, which some of our faculty attended, stressed the fact that a person is usually either a "reader" or a "listener" and that to be effective in communicating with your boss, you should determine which one he is and then primarily use that mode of communication, written or verbal, with him. A really good manager, however, would be equally effective in reading and listening since many of his subordinates, as well as superiors, will be more effective communicating one way rather than the other; and a balance will always result in better communication.

5. *Goals and Purposes.* In order for anyone to be effective or accomplish anything in life, it is necessary for him to establish some goals and a purpose in life so that he knows in which direction he is heading and what his ultimate goal will be.

Most successful businessmen that I know have established some targets in their lives and have aimed almost everything they have done toward those targets. As Christians our primary goal should be to serve Christ and win others to Him. Within this goal and purpose, however, we need to determine what means or media is most effective for us in accomplishing this goal. We can, of course, look to God for guidance in helping us determine where we fit into His plan and purpose.

One side of balance in this area would mean knowing where you are going, having confidence in what you are doing, and having your hands on the steering wheel of your life. The other side would mean seeking God's guidance each step of the way, watching for closed doors or walls that God may place in your path, and constantly looking for openings or opportunities that God has made available to you. God expects us to establish confidence and know-how in where we are going within His plan, while, at the same time, being balanced continually with a sensitivity to His guidance and redirection if necessary. "Study to show thyself approved unto God, a workman that needeth not to be ashamed. . . . prepared unto every good work" (2 Tim. 2:15, 21).

6. *Technical and Systems Comprehension.* Whatever our field of specialty, it is obviously necessary in our complex society to become technically pre-

pared for that particular vocation. We must have a comprehension of the technology involved in our profession as well as the systems and procedures that must be used to be effective. In this regard, the balance, on one hand, is being organized, prepared, exercising leadership, exercising authority. On the other hand, it is being productive, avoiding a know-it-all attitude, listening and learning, being a follower, and exercising responsibility. It's also sometimes easy to expend a great deal of effort in the wrong direction without being organized and knowledgeable. A balance here is critical also.

7. *Strengths and Weaknesses.* You must recognize your own strengths and weaknesses and apply to them the concepts of *balance* and *dynamics* (see chapter 16).

In the six areas presented above I'm sure you have noted some in which you are particularly strong and others in which you may be excessively weak. For me, personally, three have come easy, or have been my strengths, (2, 4 & 6) while the other three (1, 3 & 5) have been my weak areas which have been overcome only with a great deal of effort and difficulty. Yours will undoubtedly be different than mine. But all six of these must become strengths with both the balance and dynamics of this seventh area if we are to be effective in accomplishment, either secular or spiritual.

While these areas of preparation for an occupation are of great importance even in secular fields for anyone who would like to move ahead, they become particularly important for the Christian who is establishing a base from which he can witness. It is extremely important that a Christian be as prepared as possible for any field of endeavor. With the help and guidance, along with the strength and wisdom, of the Holy Spirit, there is no reason why a Christian cannot be prepared better than any of his contemporaries. To ignore this preparation, or to sidestep it, would be saying in effect that we do not have the guidance and wisdom available to us that we say we do in our witness for Christ.

14

Wrong—Even When Right

Early in my management career I learned a very important lesson from my dad. It was costly to me, but the Lord used it eventually to steer me into education. I might not have done that if it hadn't been for that one lesson.

Dad's real love, other than the Lord, of course, was his machines. He would design some new equipment, then follow every detail of its manufacture to make sure it was the way he wanted it. And when it came to testing a new machine, he was out in the field with the mechanics, in the dirt, mud, and grease, to find out if it was working as he intended.

On this particular day, a new machine was being tested. Dad was very busy with something else when he got the report that the machine had broken down, but no explanation was given.

At the time, I was vice-president of our company, responsible for all manufacturing, which included the equipment testing.

"Rich, the new digger has broken down; go find

out what happened to it," Dad said abruptly as he stuck his head into my office door that day.

Now, I had found that for me, at least, working through channels and delegating responsibility was a much more effective method of management than trying to run a one-man show as Dad often did. So I immediately contacted the plant manager and asked him to find out what happened and report back to me.

Down the chain of command the message went through the superintendent and the foreman involved—and back through the chain of command came the message about what the problem was. It was probably two or three hours before I got the message and I then hurried to Dad's office to fill him in.

What I didn't know was that Dad's impatience had gotten to him and he had already been out on the grade talking to the machine operator. And when my story of the problem, that I had gotten through the chain of command, didn't agree with the one he had gotten from the operator, he really began to work me over. He had expected me to go out myself and find out, and not send someone else. I tried to explain that my way of getting things done was different from his and just as effective, or more so, but he wasn't listening. He was the boss, you know!

This incident caused a breach between Dad and me that took a couple of years to heal, but eventually I realized that even though I was right (later it turned out that my story was the accurate one, the operator did not know all that had happened), I was wrong on several counts.

I learned in later years that even though I believed it strongly, there was no Scripture that says,

"Thou shalt always communicate through channels." This was an effective way for me, but not necessarily the only one.

I found that management styles must vary with individual personalities. What I considered "right" was definitely "wrong" to Dad. The Bible says, "Be not wise in thine own eyes: fear the Lord, and depart from evil" (Prov. 3:7). Also I was "wrong" because, in this case, he was the boss and he had asked me to do something which I hadn't done. Here again the Bible speaks: "Let every soul be subject unto the higher powers. For there is no power but of God: the powers that be are ordained of God" (Rom. 13:1).

The principle which I learned in this lesson is a very important one. Many of us, because of our training, may feel that things should be done in a certain way. And we may be right. Then, we may be wrong as well. God uses many different methods and people to accomplish His work here on earth and rarely, except for the *spiritual absolutes* I have dealt with earlier, can we take a dogmatic position on something when someone else has the real responsibility.

Experience has shown that in many situations involving two or more people there may be severe differences of opinion with both sides being right. Any Christian who is tempted to declare his position as the right one should always bear in mind that there are many cases of which he may not be aware where the other person may also be "right." And any declaration or enforcement of position that takes place should always allow some room for the fact that you may be wrong, even though at the moment you are certain you are right. In such a situation it is imperative that God's hierarchy of authority be recognized in the relationship with other people.

Perhaps in our vocabulary, if we could avoid using the phrase "I *know* that this is so," or "I *know* that this is the right way" and replace it with the phrase "I *don't think* that this is so" or "I *don't think* that this is the right way," we might keep our foot out of our mouth more of the time and be better able to get along with people.

You may be "right." Christ was "right" too, but on many occasions it was necessary for Him to not respond and let God carry out His purpose here on earth. Let us, you and I, also be used of God by being extremely careful how we enforce our opinion or our ways on others.

15

Ambiguous Principles

It was a typical case of marriage infidelity. The husband had had an affair, and the wife had not an inkling that anything was wrong. Later the husband, realizing the gravity of his mistake, sought counseling from his pastor. He knew the Lord as Saviour. He had sinned. He recognized this all too clearly and he wanted to be restored into fellowship with the Lord.

The pastor counseled with him, had prayer with him, and then pointed out the scriptural basis for correcting the entire situation. The first step is obvious. "If we confess our sins, He is faithful and just to forgive us our sins, and to cleanse us from all unrighteousness" (1 John 1:9).

This, of course, means asking God for forgiveness first, which God has promised to give, and then, as the pastor explained, it also means asking forgiveness of the parties that have been wronged by the sinful act and making any restitution that may be warranted.

In his case there was no restitution that could be implemented, but there were other parties that had been wronged. The wife had been wronged. The other woman had been wronged. And her husband had been wronged. Since an approach to the other husband might have resulted in violence, that was not recommended. Neither was a further contact with the other woman recommended, since she also was a guilty party and further contact might not be wise. But this pastor recommended that he had a spiritual obligation to ask forgiveness of his own wife, even though she had no knowledge of the affair.

This was a mistake! If she had knowledge of it, this certainly would have been in order, but to tell her about it in order to ask her forgiveness could create problems, and it did. It created such a rift and distrust between them that their relationship was never the same and eventually ended in separation and divorce.

In this case, there is no doubt in the minds of those who were involved that had the husband obtained forgiveness from the Lord and then had he gone quietly about renewing his relationship with his wife, even being a better husband than ever before, a wonderfully lasting relationship would have resulted. As it was, Satan used that seed of information to create a thorn in the marriage relationship that never healed.

What is the principle involved here? How and when can it be applied? This is a very delicate one, because there are scriptural principles involved that must not be violated; yet there must be an openness to the direction of the Holy Spirit in the application of these principles.

When the concepts of "grace" and "spiritual directives" collide, or seem to conflict in such a way that great harm may be done to the testimony of

Jesus Christ or His work, or that more personal harm may be done by following one concept or the other, extreme care must be exercised in which concept prevails.

These situations cannot be dealt with on a simple *spiritual absolute* basis, but must be dealt with in the same frame of wisdom that Christ used in dealing with the woman caught in adultery (John 8:3-11). There are many cases, particularly involving marriage and divorce, where to take a scripturally absolute position may be considerably more damaging to the cause of Christ and to the future of any given situation than to apply the laws of grace. And in these cases, the end certainly does not justify the means.

This concept should never be used as a "cop-out," however, and there are only a few rare cases where it is advisable to follow it. The Holy Spirit is quite capable of guiding us, however, as to when and where to apply it, if we are ever sensitive to His leading.

Without going into any details, or becoming aggressive or defensive, let me mention just four types of situations in which I feel a Christian must exercise extreme care in either passing judgment on someone else or in dealing with the situation in his or her own mind and heart.

1. When asking forgiveness of a wronged marriage partner would, as in the above case, create a wound, by exposing them to a situation of which they had no knowledge, that would be extremely difficult to heal.

2. When a divorced and remarried person is later saved, and has a happy home, to void the second marriage in an attempt to rebuild the first based solely on a supposed scriptural command. This in

many cases would be impossible. The other partner may have remarried also. It could wreck the lives of the children involved in the second marriage, to say nothing of the principle partners involved. Such a concept is not reconcilable with "grace," yet I have known of pastors who have recommended such a course of action on spiritual grounds.

3. When in a multiple-wife culture, such as encountered on the mission field, the husband is saved and then required as a condition of fellowship to divorce all except one wife. There are situations where when this is done, the released wives are rejected by their own culture 'or tribal custom, are left to fend for themselves, become prostitutes, or eventually starve to death. Yet some missionaries insist on this procedure, knowing what will result. This just cannot be God's method of correcting a situation that had been generated prior to salvation. The guidance of the Holy Spirit, with an open willingness to the alternatives, must prevail in each such situation.

4. When the freedom of choice and the equality of all people result not in real freedom but in domination by only a different power group and, with that, an almost total destruction of civilized living standards. There must be a better, God-ordained solution to the problems of black Africa than that which we have seen take place where the "white" rule has only shifted to a black radical rule which grants less freedom and less civilization than the previous white rule. The terrorist tactics of such groups, while claiming to give freedom and equality, really create greater subjection than before.

In Rhodesia and South Africa's white rule problems, Christians should be careful in taking positions. The right solution should neither (1) continue dominance and disenfranchising of blacks, nor (2) take an entire culture or economy requiring sophisticated management and give it "Robin Hood" style to black militants so that neither the whites nor blacks receive any further benefit and face, ultimately, an almost certain collapse and depreciation of all of the economy and facilities.

I don't advocate a continuance of the present status, but neither do I feel previous solutions in other black nations have been any improvement whatsoever.

God's Word is clear. When it is very specific, we should obey. Many times, however, what we think are specifics are really shades of our interpretation, and we claim them as specifics when they really are not. The guidance of the Holy Spirit is critical in these interpretations. While we ourselves may be ambiguous in our many private interpretations, the Holy Spirit will never be ambiguous if we will keep our minds and hearts open to His leading and direction in situations where the testimony and cause of Christ may open other directions that we have not previously perceived.

Part VI Six How-To's

16

How to Walk a Tightrope

While in my teens I purchased an old Model T Ford. This was in the early 1940s, when there were still large numbers of them in operation. The earlier models without a self-starter had no battery or electrical system as we know it but derived the spark for the engine from a magneto and a large number of magnets fastened to the flywheel of the engine. I remember very clearly one day when one of those magnets worked loose, causing the flywheel to be out of balance. Before I knew what was happening, the entire flywheel, including all of the other magnets, had almost totally disintegrated inside the flywheel housing. It had literally destroyed itself because of that out-of-balance condition.

Similarly our human body can be destroyed by an out-of-balance condition in the food we eat, or in the proportions of rest and activity we allow ourselves.

Perhaps we are more painfully aware of what can happen when our household economics are out of balance. When our expenditures exceed our income for a long time our economic health can be quickly destroyed.

If any one topic in this book could become a thread that would weave together all of the other topics dealt with, it would be this matter of "balance." In my previous books I have had much to say on this subject. I believe it is one of the most important that Christians fully understand. Job said, "Let me be weighed in an even balance, that God may know mine integrity" (31:6). Paul touched on the same theme: "And every man that striveth for the mastery is temperate in all things" (1 Cor. 9:25).

In the physical and technical world, balance is critical in many ways. But this is not a technical book, and my concern is more related to balance in our spiritual lives. In some very specific spiritual areas, balance is critically important and many Christians seem to have slid off to an extreme one way or the other. I am not advocating a compromise in any of these, but only an examination of emphasis to see that we are not unduly emphasizing one at the expense of the other. Here are some examples of areas where this frequently happens.

Worship vs. Service

"O come, let us worship and bow down: let us kneel before the Lord our Maker" (Ps. 95:6). Numerous other psalms, especially Psalm 100, also urge us to worship the Lord. But should we spend so much time worshiping that we have little time left to serve Him? No, because James exhorts believers to "Be ye doers of the word, and not hearers only, deceiving your own selves" (James 1:22).

I have been acquainted with some Christians who

are so busy *serving* the Lord that they just don't have sufficient time left to *worship* the Lord. And I believe worship with God's people is important too, and not just worship as an individual. What is the balance? We must do both, worship and serve, not letting one diminish the other.

Foreign Missions vs. The Local Church

We are told "Go ye into all the world, and preach the Gospel to every creature" (Mark 16:15). Yet there still is the need for someone to furnish support from the home front and a place to worship for those who cannot go. In this matter also, we have two extremes. Many who are more concerned with foreign missions will rightfully say that more money and prayer support should go to the field of service. This is true. And I would not take away at all from the urgent need for more support for the Gospel in lands abroad. But I would only caution that in a few instances, and admittedly these are very rare, such heavy emotional emphasis is given to missions that the local church becomes a financial disaster and the Lord's work is degraded because His people will not maintain the appearance of respect He commands in His Church.

A much more common problem, however, is that most Christians are so busy building a church organization and an edifice, which will give them pride as individuals rather than respect to the Lord, that they completely forget the call and the command to "go."

This problem is even more deplorable than the other extreme. My personal formula is to give half of my tithe regularly and consistently to the local church, and half to foreign missions. Your formula may need to be different—ask the Lord about it.

Any giving I do beyond the tithe is done as I see a need—to radio and TV ministries, to special missionary projects, or to other special church needs. I feel that this formula keeps me in balance.

Studies vs. Devotions
Balance here is primarily directed to our college students. Although the conflict may not be too obvious, I believe that the pressures involved in college work today by Christian students can make this a potential problem.

For a young person in college who is working parttime to pay a portion of his school costs, time becomes quite a critical factor. Attending classes, doing the required homework, holding down a job, spending time in personal devotions, and having some time left over for witnessing, relaxation, and recreation can present a difficult time problem to a dedicated Christian student. It is easy to let the pressure of studies crowd out personal devotions and relationship with the Lord.

I have also seen a case or two where extensive devotional reading has crowded out, or been used as an excuse for not doing, the school work. The result was failure of school work, and as a result, failure also in maintaining the respect of fellow students so important in maintaining an effective witness. Neither of these extremes is right, of course. A balance must be maintained and a time-allocation system devised so that both studies and devotions are pursued with equal vigor.

Witnessing vs. Job Performance
There is little need to exhort Christians to witness, for this is commanded over and over again in the Scriptures. It might be well, however, to look care-

fully at what the Scriptures say about job performance and then relate the two. Paul warned us to be "not slothful in business; fervent in spirit; serving the Lord" (Rom. 12:11). And in Proverbs we're told, "Seest thou a man diligent in his business? he shall stand before kings; he shall not stand before mean men" (Prov. 22:29).

How can these concepts of witnessing and job performance be a problem to one another? Easily! I'm sure we have all noticed some Christians who get so absorbed in their secular work that they don't have time to witness for the Lord. If we are children of God, witnessing should always be our primary emphasis. However, in order to have an effective life from which to witness effectively, we must have the respect of the people to whom we witness. They must see and recognize our authority as Christians. This is where the problem comes in. If we are haphazard or lazy in performing our secular job, and as a result fail to give our employer a fair day's work for the pay we receive, we will find it very difficult to convince others that our Christianity means something. And while some Christian employers might understand, it is seldom right to interrupt work for which we are being paid in order to witness to a fellow worker. Be a real witness to him first by the diligent manner in which you perform your job. Then he will respect you and be willing to listen to your presentation of the claims of Christ. Keep a balance between taking time to witness and your diligence in job performance.

Soft Heart vs. Hard Head

The Scriptures exhort us to have compassion on those around us. But, as mentioned in the previous item, we should also be diligent in our work and in our business affairs. While a tender heart is certainly necessary in order to have a real burden for the unsaved, it becomes necessary at times, to be hardheaded in some decisions to avoid waste of God's money and to be able to maintain a business respect. This principle applies also in many areas of the Lord's work. Christ Himself had a tender and compassionate heart in His dealing with the woman caught in adultery. But in another situation He tolerated no foolishness or disrespect in His dealings with the money-changers in the temple.

In 1965 I was involved in an unusual business proposal which my father had made to a cabinet officer in a foreign government. This man, evidently having heard of Dad's religious commitment, had assumed that because of this he might take advantage of him because he might be "soft." He remarked after reading the proposal presented to him, "I thought Mr. LeTourneau was a religious man. This proposal sounds like a businessman wrote it!"

Many people in the world of business do not feel that a soft heart and a hard head are compatible, at least not in the business world, but I feel that with Christians they must not only be compatible, but they must be carefully balanced, with real spiritual discernment as to which to apply when.

Doctrinal Complexity vs. Gospel Simplicity

As a layman I will exercise care in discussing this point, but it must be included, for I feel it is very important. Some Christian leaders I have known become so absorbed in dotting "i's" and crossing "t's" and get so bogged down in interpretations—even arguing and fighting over what the Scriptures say or don't say—that they have little time, or effectiveness, to do their primary job—winning the lost.

Many also go to the other extreme. They say that the Gospel is simplicity itself, and that to be understood by everyone it must be kept simple. They avoid all doctrine. They even gloss over the basic doctrine of the Church and, in doing so, are not able to teach new Christians the basic truths necessary to enrich their lives and help them be effective in the Lord's work. Somewhere between these two positions is a balance point. Certainly it cannot be at either extreme.

What I have attempted to convey in the matter of balance should not be construed as compromise at all. Neither am I advocating a 50/50 emphasis or split between any of these areas. Each of us must examine our own hearts and our own relationship to God, asking Him to guide us in the emphasis we place in these various areas. My purpose is to call them to your attention, lest you become an extremist on either end of the balance beams, so that you might find the most effective point of balance for your own productivity and effectiveness for the Lord.

17

How to Keep the
Pressure On

My older brother Don died in a light plane crash at age 18. He was one of those boys who seemed to be overly endowed with energy, ingenuity, and the ability to do everything that was not deemed appropriate by the older generation. Dad was a very strict disciplinarian, and Mom wasn't far behind. Don was constantly in trouble.

Even in those early years Dad was considered to be quite a successful businessman, and while we certainly didn't get anything just because we wanted it, we had all that we needed. Our spending money didn't come from allowances, either. It came strictly from earning our own money doing odd jobs, selling soda pop from a wagon to plant employees, and other enterprising tasks.

One day, in exasperation over his problems, Don complained to Mom, "Gee Mom, I know most people who have money spoil their kids rotten by giving them too much. But why does Dad have to go to the *other* extreme?"

What Don referred to is something that all of us have seen happen in families of wealth and prominence when children receive too many "wants" beyond their "necessities." Without learning the cost of obtaining these in terms of time or effort, their value system becomes distorted and they have no real challenge in life.

While teaching a college course in Human Relations several years ago, I ran into a ticklish problem. The students would always get a good laugh when I tried to talk my way out of it. The author of the textbook I was using made a flat statement that "rarely do the sons of geniuses or famous men ever amount to anything." Since my dad was both, I had some explaining to do.

While our dad could have spoiled us, he certainly made every effort to avoid it by imposing some of the strict disciplinary standards to which he had been subjected. By teaching us the value of work and of money, he taught us how to accomplish something in life. What the author of that textbook meant was that geniuses and great men rarely impose discipline on their children. Solomon wrote, "Foolishness is bound in the heart of a child; but the rod of correction shall drive it far from him" (Prov. 22:15).

If there is any one factor, other than pure mental or physical capabilities, that can determine whether a person is an outstanding success in life or a dismal failure, it is the matter of discipline. It is important *who* applies the discipline, *how* it is applied, and *why* is it applied.

Who?
Discipline can be self-imposed or can be imposed by others in a wide variety of circumstances.

1. It can be self-imposed or voluntary in temporary situations for positive reasons, such as to receive wages, earn an award, or to be accepted by others.

2. It can be self-imposed or voluntary in temporary situations because of negative reasons, such as to avoid a fine or punishment, avoid an unpleasant experience.

3. It can be self-imposed in long-term situations for either positive rewards or to avoid negative rewards by making a commitment from which it is difficult to extract oneself. Examples are enlisting for a term in the military service or enrolling in college for a term of courses.

One of the main reasons why colleges are so much more effective than home study in transmitting knowledge to students is that when a student enrolls in college he makes a long-term commitment to put himself under the disciplinary and requirement processes of study that are difficult to back out of. While a great deal of what is learned in college could be learned by checking books out of the local library and by carefully reading and studying them, few people do it because they don't have the self-discipline required to stick with it.

A student can, of course, drop out of college, too, but the discipline of avoiding the negative rewards of being classed as a dropout or a quitter frequently keeps him in the disciplined situation once the commitment is made.

God has not given us a spirit of cowardice, but of power and love and self control (2 Tim. 1:7, BERK.).

4. Discipline can be imposed on us in situations over which we have no control, such as by parents or guardians before we become of age, or by the

law or legal authorities over us. We must file income tax returns regardless of how distasteful the task might be. We must obey traffic laws on the highway and hundreds of other do's and don'ts of our structured legal society in order to avoid the consequences or punishment that would otherwise result.

5. Aside from forced discipline values, we have a multitude of pressures on us that are applied by our peers and society around us that we can accept or reject. These include the way we dress in particular places or on certain occasions, the personal habits that we develop, and the way we react to other people. All of us have a desire to be accepted, to be loved and to be respected by others, and we have a natural reluctance to be out of step or to be the oddball in a group situation. Therefore, we adopt (in most cases) the discipline of dress, habits, and personality that others expect of us in these circumstances.

How?

The Bible says, "he that ruleth his spirit (is better) than he that taketh a city" (Prov. 16:32).

The penalties that discipline inflicts can appear in an infinite number of forms, but consider three broad classifications of which one or more are involved in almost all discipline, whether self-or externally imposed.

1. *Use of time.* Time is a precious commodity to us. We are allotted a normal three score and ten (70) years on this earth. But many have significantly less than this, and only a few see too many more years. Many types of discipline consume this time which is so valuable to us. It may be sitting in the corner when we were children, it may be

studying, training or learning a skill, or an infinite variety of time-consuming activities.

2. *Requirement of effort.* For my dad when he was young, discipline may have been having to saw an extra cord of wood, which required a great deal of effort. When he became older, it was the intense studying he found necessary to comprehend an engineering concept. To an athlete it is the grueling physical training that must continue for months or years before those few seconds of achievement and recognition are reached.

3. *Unpleasant experience.* While there are other forms, the unpleasant experience is probably the most common that comes to mind when we think of discipline. For children it can be a spanking (and I received my share), or going to bed without supper. For adults this can be physical injury from disobeying highway warning signs, or could even be the spending of days or months behind bars.

Why?

A logical question that might be asked at this point in our discussion is, "Why is all discipline necessary?" For all of us and particularly for Christians, there are several very important reasons.

1. An obvious one is to avoid pain or suffering. A child must be disciplined not to touch a hot stove. Adults must discipline themselves not to use tobacco or to become alcoholics. The end result of both are pain and suffering. Whatever means we can or must use for ourselves or others can easily be accepted when the result of not using them is observed.

2. On the positive side, we must discipline ourselves in many ways if we are to reach our purposes and goals in life. No one ever achieved real success

in life without a great deal of both positive and negative discipline, both self-imposed and imposed by others. It is the difference between the Horatio Alger success story and the drifter. It's that simple.

3. The development and maintenance of health in our physical bodies requires discipline. Our activity and inactivity, what we eat and how we take care of the only physical body we'll ever have is extremely important. Ask those whose bodies have failed them due to lack of discipline. They'll tell you that if they had it to do over again no discipline would be too great to keep their physical health.

4. The development of our mental processes is also quite similar to the physical. Our minds must be exercised and developed just like our bodies if we are to obtain maximum use from them. This takes a great deal of discipline.

When Dad was a young man he would play checkers frequently with one of his friends and would consistently be beaten by him. One day he said to himself, "He's no smarter than I am and there's no reason why he should always win." With that he determined to win the next time they played. With a great deal of effort he did just that! But the exercise of his mind was so great that he lay awake all that night without sleep, his mind playing checkers all night long. He had put his mind through a new set of development exercises and it was complaining. If we are to develop our minds, then it is absolutely essential that the development processes be part of our program.

5. Character and personality must be developed also. Our ethics and our relationships with people, how we live, act, and conduct ourselves, require the application of discipline in its various forms.

6. Spiritual development is another area which many Christians fail to recognize. Many are born again into God's family but stay as babes in Christ the rest of their natural life. They never grow and mature sufficiently to enjoy the real meat of the Scripture. They're still bottle fed on the milk of the Word, even after many years. It takes discipline, either self-imposed or externally imposed. A good way to put yourself "under the gun" in this, and any other area of discipline, is to have a checkup partner. Get together with a friend, agree to and commit yourself to some goals, whether it is Scripture reading, memorizing, witnessing, or other activities. Then ask your friend to come back to you on certain dates ahead and ask how you are doing, and even nag you if necessary. It will act just like enrolling in college. To avoid the unpleasant experience of admitting that you have failed to accomplish your goals you will discipline yourself and try very hard to accomplish that to which you have made a commitment.

7. This principle applies not only to your personal Christian development but also to your outreach, your testimony, your witness, and to the image of Christ that you leave with all the other people you contact daily. If those without Christ could see a very distinct difference in the way that we Christians think, act, and conduct our lives, they would be much more anxious to know the same Christ that we know. But it takes discipline to do it.

But you say you just can't do the things we've talked about. You've tried. You've even made commitments and failed in all of them. If you know Christ you have no excuse, for He will provide the strength and the will to do what you in your own strength cannot bring yourself to do. This is where the difference lies. If we are in Christ, we can call on His unlimited strength and we need not be limited by our own human weaknesses. Accept the discipline of doing what you need to do and ask Him for the strength to do it.

18

How to Increase Your Faith through Hard Work

Faith is absolutely essential in the life of a Christian. "Without faith it is impossible to please Him" (Heb. 11:6). The word *impossible* means exactly what it says. There is no way that we can be reconciled to God and walk with Him without faith. Nothing that I say here should be construed to minimize the necessity and the importance of faith if God is to be pleased with us.

But also necessary, along with this faith and its application to our daily lives, is the need for performing the tasks God has given us to do with the wisdom and strength He has given us to do them.

Even so faith, if it hath not works, is dead, being alone. Yea, a man may say, "Thou hast faith, and I have works: shew me thy faith without thy works, and I will shew thee my faith by my works" . . . But wilt thou know, O vain man, that faith without works is dead? . . . Ye see then how that by works a man is justified, and not by faith only . . . For as the body without the spirit is dead, so faith without works is dead also (James 2:17-18, 20, 24, 26).

For the housewife to look at a kitchen sink piled high with dirty dishes and say, "Lord, I have faith that these dishes will get washed; I'm going to sit down and watch television," when she has the strength with which to wash the dishes herself, is a mockery of scriptural principles.

Dad liked to use the illustration of the two men caught in a storm in a row boat. One said, "Shall we row or shall we pray?" The other replied, "Let's do both." It's the "both" concept of works and faith that is so important for us to understand.

In my younger years I had a difficult problem coming to grips with what I felt was a presumption in my dad's faith. To me he seemed to be going blindly on in his business affairs, spending money, building machines, and taking risks that didn't appear to be good business sense. I somehow felt he was pushing his faith too far. To me this was presumption. If I had been making the same decisions he had made it probably would have been presumption. But I have learned in more recent years that it was not presumption, and the reason it wasn't was that he had the works to match the extent of his faith. Over his entire life he worked 14 to 16 hours a day, and the last 30 years of his life he spent the entire weekend, every weekend, giving his testimony for the Lord all over the world. He never really took a vacation or never really spent an evening at home in idle conversation or watching television. He had more important things to do. He was exercising the works that were necessary to validate the extent of the faith he claimed.

This concept is vitally critical in the exercise of faith. If we have little faith then perhaps we can get by with little works. If, however, we are going to exercise a great deal of faith we must also exercise a great deal of works. God has given us our body, our strength, our mind, our intellect. And He intends for us to use all of these in honoring our own faith and in honoring the faith of others.

This does not mean that God cannot perform miracles. Certainly He can and He will, but He will perform those miracles only when we are unable to accomplish the objective toward which our faith is oriented, with the strength and wisdom with which He has given His people to do them. In our modern 20th century we see few real miracles of the kind we read about in the Scripture. The miracles are really in the everyday things around us with which we can do the things that would have otherwise been a miracle centuries ago. It's not necessary that God perform a miracle for us when He has placed within our capability the ability to accomplish the goal ourselves.

A minister friend of mine told recently of an instance in his childhood where their family prayed in church for the Lord to supply food to a destitute family in the neighborhood. When they arrived home his mother began putting groceries from her own shelf in a bag, instructing the boy to deliver it to the family. She was teaching him a lesson that when we pray for someone and we have the capability of answering that prayer, God expects us to be the instrument through which that prayer is answered.

God uses His men, you and me, to carry out His work and His mission here on earth. He can provide, through His people, the food, the medicine, the money, the clothing, and whatever is needed to supply the needs represented by the faith of others of His flock. But in order for Him to do that we must be responsive to His leading and to the concept that works must accompany faith.

God is certainly able to perform physical miracles. He is able to heal, provide necessities of life, and other needs, only by exercising the power that is His. But if God did this in situations where men are capable of doing it for Him, He would rob us of both the joy and blessing that are ours in doing these things and would along with this create a laziness on our part by Him doing what we are capable of doing.

An example of the problem created when other people do for us what we are capable of doing for ourselves came to my attention several years ago. It was during a trip in behalf of our company to the United States base in Thule, Greenland, far up inside the Arctic Circle. We were told that when the government established the base there, they were careful to move all of the Eskimos a considerable number of miles away from the base. Not knowing how long the base would be there, they knew that if the Eskimos of the area became accustomed to dependence on the American personnel rather than their hard life of fishing and eking out a living in that area, they would probably become dependents of the government for their lives and for generations to come. Their present life was a hard one. It required a great deal of work. Our government feared that any lessening of this work responsibility for a period of time would make them incapable of returning to their previous work level.

If our government was so smart in that situation, I often wonder how we began to operate on such an opposite philosophy in some of our unnecessary welfare programs.

Works and faith must go hand in hand. In order to understand works we must have faith. In order to understand faith we must have works. We can have as much faith as we are willing to put works behind it. Our faith can be as weak as the weakness of the works which we are not willing to put with that faith. As Christians can absorb these principles, great and mighty things can be accomplished through both faith and works.

19

How to Get Started on the Right Foot

In the winds, rain, and floods of "change" in our society, foundations become of utmost importance. Nothing appears to be very stable any more. As a result, people everywhere are becoming frustrated and insecure. They are looking for something to hang onto. In their search and grabbing, they often turn to the occult, to pleasure, and to other satanic and worldly devices. But they are not finding in them the foundations, the stability, and the security that they need.

Yet, we all know that change must continue as it has in the past, perhaps not at as rapid a rate, but life will change nevertheless. How can we have change and yet have security? That's the problem.

Change is undoubtedly one of the most talked about and exciting subjects in our age. There is even a popular magazine dedicated entirely to the subject. It is something that has always been with us and will always be with us, but is more recognizable today than ever before in the history of man. Change is inevitable. You probably have heard many astounding statistics on this subject, but let me review just a few for you:

- Kenneth Boulding, writer and economist, says, "Half of all the energy consumed by man in the past 2,000 years has been consumed in the last 100."
- In addition he says that, "Man has extracted as much metal and materials from mines since 1910 than in all history before that."
- *Fortune* magazine a few years ago stated that: "Within a decade or two the main challenge to U. S. society will not be the production of goods, but will center around difficulties and opportunities in a world of accelerating change and ever-widening choices."
- The break between *rapid* change and *radical* change is not sharp—but can be pegged at about 1950.
- The movement is so swift, so wide, and the prospect of acceleration so great that an imaginative leap into the future cannot find a point of rest, a still picture of social order.
- Someone has also calculated that one out of four of all the people who ever lived on the earth are alive today; the volumes of technical information available to us doubles every ten years; in the world today, there are more than 100,000 technical journals published in over 60 languages and every 15 years this number doubles.

Technological Change

One important area is technological change or what might be called the technology of materials, manufacturing, communications, and transportation. The basic laws of science involved in the physical change or the foundations involved in this field are several.

There are certain laws in mathematics, such as those found in algebra, trigonometry, calculus, and differential equations, that are basic. We've compounded them; we've developed them further; we've condensed the time element necessary to use them. But the basic laws themselves have not changed.

Thirty years ago when computers were in their early stages of development, our company faced a difficult engineering problem involving the location of the bolt holes in the aluminum sheets with which we planned to build the first three-hundred-foot dome building in Longview, Texas. These holes were to be pre-drilled into each sheet, in such a precise location that when these sheets were bolted together they would automatically form the perfect sphere of the building. Each of several hundred sheets had different hole locations. Our chief engineer, using desk calculators, worked on the calculations for two solid weeks but had accomplished less than one fourth of the job. Time was running short so someone suggested using one of the newfangled computers to calculate the hole spacings. A program was written for the closest computer that was available, and with it, it only took ten minutes to solve the entire problem.

The foundation laws of mathematics, however, did not change in doing this calculation. They were simply speeded up. Even our most modern computers can actually do only very simple mathematical operations. A computer, simply "looks" at a punched card, and sees a hole or no hole in a particular location (or with a magnetic tape sees magnetic charge or no charge). It then functions according to what it has previously been programmed to do by the operator. In mathematics it cannot even add two and two. It can only add one unit at a time, putting ones together four times to get four. It is an idiot, but a high speed idiot. Yet, because of this extremely high rate of speed which it can use in adding one and one, it can perform extremely complex operations in literally a millionth of a second—in one second it can perform five million operations. Working forty hours a week, it would take 12 mathematicians 12 weeks, using desk calculators, to make these same calculations. This extremely rapid rate of calculation has permitted engineers to design aerodynamic bodies, aircraft missiles, even skyscrapers whose required calculations are so complex that it would have been impossible to design them within the life span of the designer, using only the calculators that were available 30 years ago

Medical Change
Change in the field of medicine is also significant today. In recent years there have been several attempts, with at least some degree of success, in transplanting a human heart from one body to another. This change has been a dramatic development!

One authority has estimated that 90 percent of all the drugs being prescribed by physicians today were not even in existence ten years ago and three fourths of them will be obsolete in four more years.

Many developments that were not even dreamed of five years ago are commonplace in medicine today. Medical experts have revealed that one of the biggest problems in developing practical programs today in medical education is that during the length of time it takes young people to become fully trained and to be good doctors, there has been so much advance in medical science that much of what they have learned is obsolete and out of date. Nearly all education is facing this same problem—universal lifelong education is needed.

As we look to the future in medicine, many things not only are possible but also probable. Recent medical research of our brain fluid (Deoxyribonucleic acid or DNA) which contains our memory cells and all the knowledge that we possess, and its counterpart, RNA, which contains our genetic code, has phenomenal implications. It has been calculated that it would take only a one-eighth inch cube of this fluid to store all human knowledge clear back to Adam. It also contains the genetic code and some scientists are already trying to find a way to transfer this fluid from one person's brain to another's, accumulating several life spans of knowledge in one human brain.

Scientists will continue to learn more about the human system and will learn more ways to repair and maintain the system, but the basic elements of our system of life as God designed them into our bodies must continue as they were intended to operate, without change. Our nervous system, our circulatory system, our functional system of food intake and waste disposal, and our system of intelligence are all basic foundational systems which must be maintained. Medicine can substitute or transplant specific organs and can change the outward appearance of the body, but man cannot change the basic functional systems that God originally designed and created in our bodies. Even the substitution of man-made organs within our bodies does not change the necessity of each function continuing as it was designed in our body.

Thus, even in the medical world, there are many foundations which are the basis for all change within our bodies.

Spiritual Change

But there is one critical area of change in our society today we as Christians must examine closely—spiritual change. In technology and medicine we must recognize that what man has done has sometimes resulted in death and *destruction* rather than in *construction* and life. Therefore, in preparation for our discussion in the spiritual area we need to consider I Corinthians 3:11-15. The Apostle Paul explained some important concepts to the Church at Corinth:

"And no one can ever lay any other real foundation than that one we already have—Jesus Christ. But there are various kinds of materials that can be used to build on that foundation. Some use gold and silver and jewels; and some build with sticks, and hay, or even straw! There is going to come a time of testing at Christ's Judgment Day to see what kind of material each builder has used. Everyone's work will be put through the fire so that all can see whether or not it keeps its value, and what was really accomplished. Then every workman who has built on the foundation with the right materials, and whose work still stands, will get his pay. But if the house he has built burns up, he will have a great loss. He himself will be saved, but like a man escaping through a wall of flames" (1 Cor. 3:11-15, LB).

Note that the main part mentioned is the foundation. There may or may not be a permanent and lasting structure built on it and, of course, there may or may not be a reward resulting.

The parallels which I am attempting to develop should be clear. I'm sure there is a relationship of the spiritual area to the technical and medical areas we have been discussing.

First of all, our solid foundation on the solid Rock, Christ Jesus, is the absolutely vital starting point for any change in the spiritual realm. The basic truths of God's Word, the basic plan of salvation, the necessity of being born again, trusting and having faith in God, are all foundations which must be maintained, if we are to develop an effective and mature witness to others around us.

The methods, however, that we utilize in our life and witness may be subject to change. In fact, with time they must change. The equipment and resources that we use may also change; in fact they must also change. These must keep pace with progress elsewhere in the world. As Christians, we can and should take advantage of the advances that are available to us—computers, medicine, education, history, psychology, even management philosophy. If we don't learn to use them there will be masses who otherwise could be reached that will not be reached with the Gospel.

Thirty years ago it was humanly impossible to reach every person in the world with the Gospel of Christ. Today all that has changed. We have a much greater knowledge of linguistics. We now have the capability of reducing any language in the world to writing within a matter of weeks. We even have developed computer programs to aid in this process. We have high speed printing presses that can turn out thousands of Bibles per hour. We have jets and helicopters, for both material and personnel, that can reach the most remote parts of the earth. We have radio transmitters that can blanket the earth with the Christian message. Far East Broadcasting, HCBJ in Ecuador, Trans World Radio, ELWA in Liberia, and many more are now reaching entire nations never touched before with the Gospel message in their own language.

There are many more avenues available to us that have not yet been utilized but which should be, in spreading the Gospel. If satellites can transmit the Olympic Games on TV, live from overseas within a short period of time, we should be able to use some of these same technological advances to present the Gospel to the darkest parts of Africa, South America, or Asia.

There are also opportunities for business establishments in many countries in which missionaries are not permitted and through which we can have the opportunity to develop a real Gospel witness. It may surprise you to see the way our mission emphasis is going to change within the next couple of decades, should the Lord tarry. We have already proved that a layman dedicated to a life of service and witness for the Lord within his own profession can be a very effective means of reaching people for Christ. If we as Christians and as laymen do not find some way to use this principle more effectively with the yet millions of unreached, we will have failed to use the knowledge and the technology that is available to us today to win souls for Christ.

Modern mission work is currently undergoing change. And it must continue to change even more rapidly.

But our foundations on which these changes are built must continue to be the real foundations provided for us in the Scripture. These foundations alone can provide the stability and security in a rapidly changing world. Our own nation, particularly, must recognize this need for continuing to build only on this foundation.

If my people, which are called by my name, shall humble themselves, and pray, and seek my face, and turn from their wicked ways; then will I hear from heaven, and will forgive their sin, and will heal their land (2 Chron. 7:14).

Let's get back on the right foundation in our personal lives, in our institutional affairs, and in our governmental affairs, and perhaps God will continue to bless our nation as He has in the past.

20

How to Worry about Worry

One of Dad's favorite stories about worry was about an unmarried lady standing by a well crying. When someone asked why she was crying, her reply was, "I was just standing here thinking that someday I might get married, have a child, and that the child might fall in this well and drown."

How amusing and ridiculous it was for her to be concerned about a chain of events that remote or that far off. Yet, I'm sure our Heavenly Father might be just as amused at us the way we agonize ourselves over things that are just as remote or just as far off when put within the context of Scripture.

Worry is a tough problem for many people, but one over which others have complete victory. I'm convinced, though, that this depends more on the personality and emotions in many of us and that there are just some to whom this is just naturally not really a problem. Those who are more sensitive to people, or who have a basic insecurity, seem to have more trouble with worry than others. Some have a natural, happy-go-lucky attitude about everything in life or perhaps believe strongly in predestination and are able to shrug off these feelings of anxiety or worry.

To those who have a problem with worry, the Scripture is very clear. The verses quoted below are only a start. We need to remember that God is always in control. Nothing happens that He does not permit. As long as we are in a close walk with Him, and are trusting fully in Him, we can always take our burdens, our anxieties, and our worries to the Lord and *leave* them there. I know it's not as easy as it sounds but it can and should be done. Paul wrote, "Don't worry about anything; instead pray about everything; tell God your needs and don't forget to thank Him for His answers" (Phil. 4:6, LB).

Now this verse doesn't mean that we shouldn't be diligent in our planning, in our work, and in whatever way we need to be doing something to make it more difficult for our fears to be realized. God always expects us to put works with our faith and do our part in bringing about or avoiding the thing we are concerned about. But after we have done our best, all we know to do, then we must claim the promises of His Word.

If you haven't done your best in your job and the boss reprimands you for it, maybe you *should* worry about getting fired. And perhaps that worry will cause you to improve your performance. Don't misuse God's promises by saying, "I'm not going to worry, God won't let him fire me," and then go on with a halfway performance in your job.

Likewise, don't expect God to provide security for you in your old age if you have a good income, are constantly wasteful of your money now, and have not set any aside for the future. Here again, maybe you *need* to worry so you'll keep your affairs in better order. When Christ said to "take no thought for the morrow" (Matt. 6:34), I think He was saying that if we use good sense in planning and doing what's right for today, then He will take care of tomorrow. But if we are careless with today, then we have no right to expect Him to cover up for us in His provision for tomorrow.

But a word of caution is in order to those who may be a little smug because they are never anxious or never worry. Unless you have been prone to worrying in the past and the Holy Spirit has helped you conquer it, you probably have no idea how difficult it is to overcome. If your personality and emotions are such that worrying has never really been a problem to you, then be careful how you judge others and flippantly suggest that "all they have to do is trust the Lord." Christ, Himself, was overcome with human emotion when His close friend Lazarus had died, even though He knew that He would raise him to life again. But that didn't keep Him from having human feeling and sorrowing with those He was with.

So before you criticize someone else, remember that it is their real feeling and concern that often makes them appear anxious and as the expression goes, "that's not *all bad*."

But isn't it wonderful that the Holy Spirit can give us that precious balance in our emotions and logic so that we can emphathize with others, show our love and concern, and be diligent in all our affairs without having the anxiety and fear that would make a mockery of God's promises. "Let Him have all your worries and cares, for He is always thinking about you and watching everything that concerns you" (1 Peter 5:7, LB).

21

How to Deal
with Dichotomies

To the undiscerning, many of the commands given
to us as Christians may appear to be in conflict
with one another. At least in the natural sense these
commands seem to be tugging on our emotions in
different directions. Some of these are dealt with
in the chapter on "Walking the Tight Rope." And
that exhortation deals with the need to avoid extremes with regard to some of these apparently
conflicting demands on our time and emotion. This
chapter moves a step deeper into God's truth to
show why in many of these areas we should *not*
find a balance point. Sometimes we should instead
pursue both to the fullest, even though they appear
to be in opposite directions. This is not possible in
the natural man, but then we have more than just
natural power available to us, don't we? One of
these dichotomies is the need to be zealous and to
have humility at the *same time*.

Humility is probably one of the most misunderstood of the qualities of the dedicated Christian.

To most people humility has a connotation of weakness or timidity, but that is really not what the term means, at least not in the spiritual sense. Humility really means the opposite of pride, or the ability to remove any selfishness or self-exposure from the scene. Humility certainly does not preclude being aggressive or active, as long as it is not a projection of self. How is that done? It can be done through projecting Christ and in keeping our own need for recognition or approval in the background. When Peter had healed the lame man in the temple (Acts 3:2-12), and the people began to respond to Peter in a way that would tend to puff up his self-image, he responded with perfect humility. He said in effect, "What are you looking at us for? We didn't do anything. The Lord did it!"

Peter was certainly not a timid person. Neither was he inactive. He was very zealous and aggressive—even sometimes impulsive. Yet he exhibited real humility in setting forth Christ as the One who performed the miracle, not himself. This is, in effect, a zealous humility, and the way we as Christians should act. Not a balance between being timid and aggressive, but being both and *at the same time*. We can be timid in relation to self and aggressive in relation to Christ. This zealous humility is really a dual thrust, rather than a dichotomy, which is capable of action in two apparently different directions, through the power and discernment which are available to us through the Holy Spirit.

A numerical or percentage analogy may clarify this concept. Let's say that 100 percent is the ultimate that we can exercise in "faith," if we had no "works" at all, and 100 percent is the ultimate that we could perform in works, if we had no faith at all. To arrive at a balance in our lives between faith and works we might be tempted to exercise a 50 percent level in faith and perform a 50 percent level in works. That might be a good balance, but that's not good spiritual dynamics. With the guidance of the Holy Spirit available to us and His power and strength also available, there is no reason why we can't both exercise a 100 percent level in faith and perform a 100 percent level in works *at the same time*. Like the men caught in a storm in a row boat, we can both row and pray at the same time and at our full spiritual capacity. The application of this type of spiritual dynamics is the only way to really deal with this dichotomy.

Thus, with the proper spiritual perspective we can exercise this "faith-works" and "zealous-humility" as though they were twins in both body and mind, and with complete isolation between the twins. This is possibly only with God's discernment, however, since our human mind and body cannot comprehend this.

Many people have a problem with predestination, or the foreknowledge of God, as it relates to their lives and their future, compared with the free will God has given us to choose our life's course and to accept or reject Him. If God had a human mind, He couldn't do this because the human mind cannot separate the foreknowledge of an event and the free will to alter it. But God does not have a human mind; His mind is divine. He can leave the course of events to our own free will to change them, knowing what we will do, but not committing us to any pattern or interfering with that free will. This same divine capacity is available to us to make possible the dual dynamics we are discussing. Let's look at a few other examples briefly.

Acceptance and Perseverance

We discussed this question thoroughly in another chapter, but it is a good example of a dichotomy. We must learn to accept where God has put us and what He has given us and, *at the same time,* we must persevere to change and expand our opportunities. Only with the power of the Holy Spirit working in us can we give the proper commitment to both concepts without our human minds confusing them.

Being Logical and Being Led of the Spirit

Many people look for a direction from the Lord that is unusual or illogical just so they can recognize it as not being their own emotions and so that they can impress others that this was a revelation from God and not just using their good sense. While this may happen, and God may open or close doors that are illogical, I am convinced that it is wrong to *seek* such avenues of direction. God created our minds and He is capable of using logic better than we are. Except in rare cases, or where it is obvious that God has intervened, we should consider that the logic that God has given us or placed in our minds *is* the leading of the Spirit. If we are in a close walk with Him, we can exercise the spiritual dynamics of using logic and good sense and being guided by the Holy Spirit *at the same time.*

Softhearted and Hardheaded

We are exhorted in the Scriptures to love and have compassion for our fellow man (John 13:35; 15:12). Yet we are also exhorted in the Scriptures to be diligent in business (Rom. 12:11), and to remove from our fellowship any who commit sin in our midst (1 Cor. 5). How can this be? It can't be in the mind and emotions of the natural man, but with the perception available through the Holy Spirit, it is not only possible but it is necessary. If it is necessary to deal harshly with someone else in our business or in our fellowship, we can still use our spiritual dynamics and do it with love and compassion. Neither does our love or compassion need to dictate giving away or throwing away the funds or goods God has entrusted to our care. Just as it is not always wise to express our love for our children by giving them everything, so it may not be wise between adults either. God can and will give us the discernment and judgment to make these decisions and to carry them out with both compassion and diligence *at the same time*.

All of this presupposes, of course, that we are born again into the family of God, have accepted Christ as personal Saviour and Lord of our lives and are committed to His will and His work in all that we do. If you qualify in this, you can deal with these dichotomies and use the spiritual dynamics that are available to you to work miracles in your effectiveness for Him.

Part VII Seven Questions

22

Who's Boss around Here?

Have you ever heard the question, "Who's in authority around here?" or the statement, "I don't have the authority to do that!", or possibly even the complaint, "Why do I have to submit to his authority?" What is authority, really? How is it obtained? From whom do we get it, and how can it be used most effectively?

A great deal of humor centers around whether the husband or the wife is the boss, and in some cases this conflict turns into heartache as well. The same is true between parents and children. Do parents really have authority over their children? Some child psychologists would even argue in favor of the children.

But God's Word is very clear about this matter of authority and the hierarchy or levels of submission involved. Let's first examine three basic concepts concerning the existence of authority and the hierarchy involved and then identify three types of authority that exist both in the secular and the spiritual realms.

All authority comes from and originates with God.
God is the supreme authority over all. "There is
no power but of God: the powers that be are ordained of God" (Rom. 13:1).

Next in the sequence or levels of authority, we
have earthly rulers, or government and the authority delegated by it. On the job, we have the person
or organization by whom we are employed. At
home the husband is the head of the house and
then in sequence are the wife and the children.

It must be understood that God normally works
through these various levels of authority and not
around them. Only when it is clear and unmistakable that the authority over us in this chain of
command is directing us to do something contrary
to specific scriptural commands, do we as Christians have the right to disobey.

"Jesus answered, [to Pilate] 'Thou couldst have
no power at all against Me, except it were given
thee from above'" (John 19:11).

Authority is dependent on submission.
This concept, of course, requires ultimate submission to God and His individual plan for us and to
His plan for the ages. If we refuse to submit to the
next level of authority above us, we have no right-
ful authority available to us to carry out our own
work and functions in life. The effect of this concept appears in its most damaging form in the home
when the father does not submit to the authority
of God or even the authority of his employer. When
this happens he undermines the authority that he
would have over the wife or over the children.

In the same manner, when the wife does not submit to the authority of the husband, she loses her
ability to exercise authority over the children. But,

you say, why should that affect the authority that rightfully belongs to us? The third concept answers this question.

No authority exists unless it is accepted.

Acceptance of authority is really submission. It is strictly voluntary. To not accept may be wrong. It may even be sin. But God has given us a free will, and no one is under authority unless he accepts it. Children rebel. Teenagers leave home. College youths may riot. By not accepting authority over them, the authority ceases to exist. For this reason authority must be obtained and exercised in such a way that it will be accepted by others. This brings us to the ways in which authority can be received and how that affects its use.

First is the authority of *position*. Such authority is given to us by a superior when we are given a job to do. In our company this authority was given to me by the Board of Directors when they elected me as president. Faculty members in our college have this authority of position in the classroom because the dean has given it to them when they were assigned that class.

In the armed services, authority is normally related to the rank held. A captain has a certain level of authority. This is his authority of position. A colonel, a lieutenant, a sergeant, or a corporal also has a certain amount of authority because of his position.

Even the authority of the husband in the home is first of all an authority of position. This authority of position is necessary in many cases but it's a rather poor kind of authority to use by itself, and relying on it alone is where most of us get into trouble with authority.

A second kind of authority is much more desirable to use. It is the authority of *knowledge*. Authority of knowledge is not given to you by a superior. Authority of knowledge is self-acquired. You have it because you've studied or you have exposed yourself to experience and, therefore, you have knowledge of a particular area or function. Those who are working under you will recognize your authority because you know what you are doing. It must be coupled with the authority of position but when it can be added, the former need not be relied upon.

Having the knowledge and experience necessary for your job makes employees more willing to accept your authority. Because it generates a greater willingness to accept than the authority of position might generate by itself, it is a better and more effective kind of authority. A parent, who speaks from experience and knowledge in using authority over the children, will find it much more acceptable than the authority of position which may say, "I am your father, you do what I say!" But the authority of knowledge may still not be sufficient to generate a necessary acceptance level. There is yet another kind of authority even more desirable.

It is the authority of *esteem* or *respect*. It is not given to you by your boss or superior. Neither can you give it to yourself by extensive preparation. This is given to you by your associates, by those who work for and with you. It also must be coupled with the authority of position, but when you have generated this kind of authority, you have less need to rely on authority of position and you can accomplish much more. With this kind of authority you can do your best job.

By gaining the authority of esteem and respect

from the men in your business organization, in addition to your authority of position and knowledge, you are really able to get things done. If foremen, supervisors and management in all levels of a business could learn to develop this kind of authority over their people, production would increase.

When an officer in the armed services is able to generate the respect and esteem of his men, only then can he become a good leader. Similarly in the home, when the father and mother have the respect and esteem of their children in addition to the authority of position and knowledge, then the children's acceptance of that authority becomes complete and a harmonious relationship can develop.

We have all seen children do things for a parent or relative whom they respect while, at the same time, rebelling strongly at doing the very same things for one they do not respect.

For these reasons the authority of esteem or respect is certainly the most desirable. While the other two types of authority must also be present, the less they need to be used the better.

Authority of position, authority of knowledge, authority of esteem or respect—the first is given to you by your superior or those over you in the hierarchy of authority, the second is acquired by yourself, the third is earned from your associates or those below you in the hierarchy of authority.

These concepts can apply to Christian living. As Christians we have the first kind of authority, of position, because we are born again. This spiritual authority, just like authority given to you in a job, must first be accepted. If a manager's position is offered to you, you must either accept it or reject it. You can't be a manager if you won't accept the job. The same is true in our Christian lives. We have the authority of position given to us by God only if we accept Christ as our Saviour.

But then, this authority alone is not sufficient to do our work for Christ effectively. If this is the only authority we have, we will not be able to do very much for the Lord. We will be like the manager at the plant who has only authority of position. He wouldn't be able to get much done. In our spiritual lives, we must generate the second kind of authority—the authority of knowledge. We must store in our minds and hearts a knowledge of God's Word and the spiritual truths that it contains. Our competence in handling God's Word will cause people to accept our testimony. Peter tells us, "But sanctify the Lord God in your hearts: and be ready always to give an answer to every man that asketh you a reason of the hope that is in you with meekness and fear" (1 Peter 3:15). If we as Christians can capture this second kind of authority, the authority of knowledge of God's Word, we can then be "ready always" and people will listen to us.

But that's still not enough authority. Many Christians, even some prominent Christian leaders, sad to say, rest only on the first two authorities. The third kind of authority, authority of spiritual respect or esteem, is also important. This kind comes only through maturity, judgment, discernment, and the life which we exhibit before others, a life that gains the respect and esteem of associates.

One example of this kind of authority stands out to me. Billy Graham has no more authority of position that you or I have, if we have accepted Christ and are born again. There are also probably hundreds of men over the country who are more knowledgeable in theology, in the Scriptures, in experience and in dealing with people, and who thus have as much or more spiritual authority of knowledge than Dr. Graham. His sermons are very simple. They're not complicated in theology or in doctrine. Then what makes him so effective in his ministry? It comes from this third kind of authority —that of respect and esteem. Through his close communion with the Lord, his discernment, his dedication, his maturity in dealing with people, he has gained the esteem and respect that causes literally millions of people, including kings and presidents, to listen to him.

Many prominent Christian men have little, if any, of this third kind of authority because they have failed to realize its importance and have not gained a real respect from their people. They have missed this ultimate requirement for Christian authority. Many have literally destroyed this authority in their own ministry by letting a lack of judgment or discernment get them into open fights or arguments with other leaders, losing spiritual respect as a result.

In spiritual matters, just as in secular matters, we must recognize and accept authority. The first, position, is absolutely necessary; the second, knowledge, is also necessary; but the third, respect or esteem, is the most important if our lives are to count for the Lord. Paul told Titus, "These things speak and exhort and rebuke with all authority. Let no man despise thee" (Titus 2:15).

Paul spoke of "our authority, which the Lord has given us for edification, and not for your destruction" (2 Cor. 10:8). Let's make sure we have developed this best kind of authority in our lives both in the secular and spiritual realms, so that others will accept our authority and lives will be changed.

23

What Do You Think I Am, a Heathen?

The term *Christian* today seems to have taken on a meaning which in many cases is considerably more broad in scope than its initial application to the disciples at Antioch. "They assembled themselves with the church . . . and were called Christians" (Acts 11:26).

Because of the broad usage of the word *Christian,* many misunderstand what a Christian really is. If several people were asked the question, "Are you a Christian?" there would be a variety of affirmative answers.

1. "Of course I am! What do you think I am, a heathen?" To many people the term Christian is used only to differentiate between civilized and uncivilized people, classifying all the civilized world as Christian. This obviously is a misnomer. While Christians tend to be more civilized than many other groups, the concept that all who live in a civilized society are Christians, when they have no relationship with Christ, is certainly a misuse of the term.

2. "Oh, yes, I have rejected my tribal African culture and have become a Christian." Many missionaries say that this very dangerous concept is a very difficult one to deal with in witnessing to people in a different culture. They look at Western society as basically Christian. They see all of the advantages and material welfare that are offered by this Christian society. Then they look at their tribal culture and the little that it has to offer in any way. So when the offer is extended to them to become Christians, many are eager to accept for two reasons: the material advantages that they perceive might be gained by becoming Christians, and second, because they have been taught to do what the foreigner asks them to do, out of courtesy, even though they don't understand it.

Several years ago a Liberian student accepted Christ while working in our industrial missionary project in Liberia, West Africa. He was a model Christian, and a couple of years later he enrolled in LeTourneau College in Texas with high recommendations from those who knew him in Liberia. Shortly after his coming, however, he began to get into difficulty when he developed desires for conveniences he couldn't afford. He was later fired from his job for dishonesty. In dealing with this student, I attempted to get to the root of his problem by discussing with him why he couldn't do these things as a Christian and as one who had accepted Christ as his personal Saviour. Out of our discussion came the fact that he had never really accepted Christ. He had viewed Christianity as a cultural change, as rejecting his African culture, adopting the Christian culture, and then attempting to fit into that culture by agreeing to everything anyone asked him to do in regard to it, and by learning all of the clichés that go along with it. For several years those around him thought that he had accepted Christ into his life, when actually he had not.

3. "Sure, I'm a member of the First denominational church." How often have you heard an answer like this when asking someone if he is a Christian? If you listen carefully you'll notice sometimes he says he is a *member* of that church and does not say he *attends*. Church membership to many has become a substitute for true Christianity. And many have falsely joined a church, thinking the act gave them a religious status as a Christian, while having no real perception of what it means to accept Christ as Saviour.

4. "Yes, I was baptized when I was three years old." Baptism, whether as a baby or when a person joins the church, is an act of public profession or dedication but is not the act of acceptance of Christ as Saviour. Many misconstrue baptism as being the ritual through which they can become a Christian.

5. "Sure I attend Sunday School and church every Sunday." Even Sunday School, as valuable as it is in Christian training, does not validate an individual's status as a Christian. I have heard personal testimonies of men, one of whom had been a Sunday School superintendent for years, who had never accepted Christ as their personal Saviour. It's not the action in which we get involved. It's the act of accepting Christ.

6. "Yes, I accepted Christ as my Saviour when I was 10 years old." Now the answers are beginning to mean something. Christianity must be related to Christ, not just to the church, to a ritual, to a culture or society, but to Christ Himself. It is an

individual act, a personal act, having nothing to do with the church or ritual. These can follow the act or decision, but should never be misconstrued as being the qualification for acceptance of Christ. But then let's go even one better with an answer to our question.

7. "Yes, I've been born again; the Lord is precious to me, and I walk with Him daily." That is an answer deserving of the term Christian. Nearly forty years ago a speaker conducted a contest for a definition of What Is a Christian? (in twenty five words or less) in the high school I was attending. The first prize was "A Christian is one who believes on Christ, confesses Him, and does His work joyfully."

Let's use the term Christian in its proper sense—a person who has a personal relationship with Jesus Christ, and then let's make sure that those around us know what that term really means.

24

Christians Can Be the Best Workers, but Are They?

As we work, do our shopping, or otherwise move through the activities of each day, we may not be aware of it, but the way we conduct ourselves is being carefully observed by someone. The Christianity displayed by the little things we say and do may be the only Christianity some know.

A Christian in a work situation, where he can be observed by his fellow workers who are not Christians, has a particularly heavy responsibility in representing Christ.

What you do Monday through Friday on your job can be many times more important than what you do on the Lord's Day. Attitudes toward your work, and toward your company, attitudes toward your boss, attitudes toward your family and yourself all will be seen much more clearly by your associates in your job than they will by your fellow church members. And how much more important it is that non-Christians see you in a life that is desirable and enjoyable so that they will want to investigate what makes you different from others.

Since the Holy Spirit working in us makes available to us a compensating power that can overcome any negative forces we might encounter in our daily activities, we should be able to exhibit to our fellow workers a great example of what Christianity can do for them. But how can we do that?

I have worked in and around factories all my life. While most of my experience has been in a company owned and operated by Christian men, still the organization was so large and so complex that there were large numbers of people involved who made no pretense of Christianity. Through the years I have had close association with men of these attitudes, and do you know what "turns them off" from looking further into Christianity? You guessed it! It's the Christians they work with.

They don't have the advantage of knowing how well we perform and behave on the Lord's Day among our fellow Christians. They miss out completely on how pious we can be then, how beautifully we pray, or the testimony we give in the Sunday night service. They don't even give us points for being in prayer meeting on Wednesday night and they don't hear the words that we say for Christ on the job, if we say them at all.

What they do see and observe, though, is what we say about our job, our company, and our boss. They also observe whether or not we do our job well and faithfully. And they observe whether or not we steal from our employer.

Steal? A Christian steal? Yes! That's what I said. Steal! It may be only pencils or a roll of tape; then again it might be considerably more, or it might be the time that you waste, your own time or the time of others.

Remember, if you are being paid by the hour or for a certain portion of a day, your time has been purchased by your employer. It no longer belongs to you. If you use it for your own benefit rather than for his, that's just the same as stealing money from him. Even witnessing to a fellow worker on your employer's time is, in effect, stealing money from him.

So what "turns others off" about the Christ you supposedly represent? They may not see any difference in you from the others working along with you who do not know Christ. If you don't act any differently from the others, then what reason could they have for wanting to investigate further what it's all about? "Let your light so shine before men, that they may see your good works, and glorify your Father which is in heaven" (Matt. 5:16).

How well we do our job, how well-prepared we are for it, and our attitudes toward everyone concerned with it are many times more important to our testimony than our presence and piety on Sunday. We really don't have to "say" a lot either. We just need to perform our job in such a manner and with such an attitude that our fellow workers will say, "He is a really great guy. I wish I could be like him. I wonder what makes him tick?"

Once this testimony and job performance have been established then you probably will have the opportunity to tell them what really makes you tick. But until you establish that kind of job reputation you'll do the cause of Christ a favor if you'll keep your mouth shut about being a Christian.

"Don't tell people I'm a Christian?" Yes, that's what I said. If you're not going to live it, don't talk it. This is what I meant earlier. Many men I have talked with in our factories will have nothing to do with the Church or Christianity. They are completely turned off because they hear Christians talking about Christ and they see no results or no difference in the way they do their job.

If we could devise a filter for our mouth that wouldn't let any words come out that are not backed up by our actions and our attitudes, Christianity would be a giant step ahead. The chorus we used to sing says it just about as well as it can be said:

What you are speaks so loud
That the world can't hear what you say.
They're looking at your walk,
Not listening to your talk,
They're judging by your actions every day.
Don't believe you'll deceive
By claiming what you've never known.
They'll accept what they see,
And know you to be,
They'll judge from your life alone.

The sad thing about this lack of performance of many Christians on their job is that it is not necessary. We have resources of strength and wisdom not available to those outside of Christ, yet we so frequently do not use them. We rely on only our human strength and are overcome by human weaknesses as we plod along in our own weak way, "striving" to do what is right. Paul wrote, "For I am not ashamed of the Gospel of Christ, for it is the power of God" (Rom. 1:16).

Let's get out from "under the circumstances." Let's get on top of them. Let's claim the strength and the wisdom that are available and then let's perform our job in such a way that we'll be a real shining witness for Christ without ever having said a word.

25

The Day of Rest?
Are You Kidding?

Working and other physical activities on Sunday, whether they be job related, home related, or even sports related have been a perennial problem to many Christian people. The Scripture appears to be very clear on what should be our attitude toward this day that is set aside for rest and for worship. "Remember to observe the Sabbath as a holy day . . . On that day you are to do no work of any kind" (Ex. 20:8, 10, LB). Yet, Christ Himself was accused of not "keeping" the Sabbath or of "working" on the Sabbath when he healed the lame man.

"Jesus told him, 'Stand up' . . . Instantly the man was healed . . . But it was on the Sabbath . . . So they began harrassing Jesus as a Sabbath breaker" (John 5:8-16, LB).

Among equally devout Christians you will find a very wide range of opinions on what is and what is not permissible to do on Sunday. For me to attempt to list the do's and the don'ts as I see them would convince some people that I am a prude and others that I am a liberal. Not wishing to be labeled and pigeonholed, even though this may be wishful thinking after reaching this point in the book, I will try only to show you factors you must take into consideration in making evaluations, as they might apply to yourself, or judgments, as they might apply to others.

1. In a complex society, there are many support services that must function on Sunday and that even Christians can't do without. These include the local fire department, police, production of electric power, functioning of telephones, natural gas for heating and cooking, water supply, institutional food services such as a college cafeteria, hospitals, ambulances, and even the church nursery. To be able to do without these functions and services, we would need to go back to a very primitive society. Yet it takes hundreds of thousands of people to provide these services for Christians as well as everyone else. Is it a good testimony for the Christianity we represent for us to refuse to perform such services on Sunday, thereby causing a fellow worker or neighbor, to whom we are a witness, to do this work for us?

2. There are many other support services in our society that Christians *could* do without but which society cannot do without. These include restaurants, gas stations, airlines, buses, trains, mail movement, business security personnel, radio and television stations, or even a taxicab ride to church. Here again, if we as Christians utilize these services, we are causing others to work on Sunday and may be keeping them out of God's house. And even if we don't use these services, society depends on them and someone must do the work.

A pastor, in whose home I was having Sunday

dinner several years ago, told me that he never "eats out" on Sunday—at least not any more. Early in his ministry, he would eat at a certain restaurant regularly for the noon meal on Sunday with his family. One day in his desire to be a witness to the waitress, he invited her to his services the next week.

"I can't come, preacher. I have to work every Sunday," was her reply.

"Tell your boss you want off next Sunday," my friend encouraged.

"Then, who'd feed you?" she logically responded.

That remark burned so deeply into the heart of that pastor that he resolved never again to eat in a restaurant on Sunday if it could at all be avoided.

3. Another part of our complex industrial society of today, if we attempted to shut down on a Sunday each week, would become prohibitively expensive and very impractical. Included in this category are the steel mill blast furnaces, the chemical plants and refineries, and ocean shipping. Without these in continuous operation, even on Sunday, we would not be able to have the cars, homes, clothes, and various other products of our standard of living at the level we now have them. In this category again, someone must work to keep these processes in operation. Should the Christians do it? Should Christians involved in business refuse to take part in these activities? This is another question you must answer for yourself.

4. In the last two items we should deal with motives for working on Sunday. If our motives are good, not primarily related to additional monetary gain, or so that we can have time for other activities on other days, then perhaps that should be a consideration. Many categories of Sunday work may

be the only employment that can be obtained, as in the case of teenagers. It may also be the case for an unemployed person striving to earn a living for his family. Also, some essential work might be done by Christians if their motive in doing it is to permit others, who might be required to work, to attend worship services. Don't forget that for your pastor, the hardest day's work of his week is on Sunday. Yet few question this because of the necessity of it and the motives for which he is doing it.

5. Since it is an individual decision, obviously many will choose not to involve themselves in an occupation that requires Sunday work. And this would probably be the case for the majority of us. But then what is our motive for *not* working on Sunday? Is it to be a testimony to others, to encourage them, to protect the Lord's Day as a Holy Day and a day of rest? Or is it for selfish or self-righteous reasons. By not working we may cause others to have to work and even this could raise a cloud over our Christian testimony.

Should you work on Sunday? That is still a question you will need to answer. I trust that in answering it, you have been made to think a little more carefully about the involvements of your relationships to other people as you make this decision.

26

Are You Always Finding Fault?

It has always been a mystery to me why some people, who claim the power of God working in their lives, seem to be so unhappy and constantly so critical, finding fault and complaining about everything around them. As Christians we are to lead victorious lives. We are to work in harmony with our fellow Christians. Yet it seems we spend more time and energy bickering and quibbling than in our witnessing for Christ. This constant attitude of criticism detracts from our testimony in the eyes of those to whom we are witnessing.

In business situations, even aside from Christianity, we have the same problems. On many occasions it has been necessary for me to discuss with managers and executives the need to develop a perspective on the importance of things that might disturb them in relationship to the job to be accomplished. I call it "relativity of importance."

The problem is that the degree of attention we give a matter is more related to our emotional involvements than to the practical or real importance of that matter. One of the secrets of getting along with people is to learn how to use this relativity of importance. If we can learn to yield to others on matters that are not really important, even though we may have an emotional involvement of "principle," and stand firm only on matters that are genuinely important, we will be surprised at how well we get along with people. The matters which may be only emotional to us may really be important to others, and the matters which are really important to us may not be that important to others. For these reasons if we can learn to subjugate ourselves to this principle we'll find that many disagreements and arguments will melt away.

This same concept carries over very heavily into Christianity. Someone has said, "No one has ever been won to Christ by arguing with him." Engaging in an argument with someone to whom we are witnessing almost is a reversal of the "importance" principle I just mentioned. If we can learn to love people for what they are and put our doctrinal shades of difference and our quibbling behind us, by not arguing, but loving and winning through the guidance of the Holy Spirit, we can be much more effective in our witness. The ultimate in the ridiculous extent to which some of us carry our opinions might be illustrated by the story of a man who was so premillennial that he wouldn't let his wife buy Post Toasties for the breakfast table.

Some people seem to feel that they have been "called" by God to tear down, correct, or criticize other Christians or Christian organizations. Such a "calling" really makes a mockery of the love of Christ. If we really want to help a person or an organization, we should pray for them, love them, and counsel them in a kind way. Public criticism or an attempt to force changes outside of God's ordained channels of authority are just *not* in keeping with scriptural principles.

I have encountered persons in Christian organizations on many occasions, who, while they have not themselves submitted to God's hierarchy of authority, have (unscripturally) taken to themselves the task of tearing down the organization in which they serve. And when this happens they generally have many followers who do not understand either the concepts of authority or the concepts of quibbling and the Lord's work suffers greatly as a result. Paul addressed this problem:

> That ye put off concerning the former conversation the old man, which is corrupt according to the deceitful lusts; And be renewed in the spirit of your mind; And that ye put on the new man, which after God is created in righteousness and true holiness . . . Let all bitterness, and wrath, and anger, and clamour, and evil speaking, be put away from you, with all malice: And be ye kind to one another, tenderhearted, forgiving one another, even as God for Christ's sake hath forgiven you (Eph. 4:22-24, 31-32).

We Christians should learn to differentiate between the important basic Gospel truths and the less important variant interpretations. If we could learn to work with people in a harmonious humble spirit without dissension, discord, or an unyielding spirit, we could accomplish a great deal for God and His kingdom in our relationships with both fellow Christians and the unsaved to whom we are witnessing.

27

Are You a Joiner?

A perplexing question which often confronts a Christian concerns which activities or organizations he can join or associate with without compromising his Christian testimony. We have been placed *in* the world by Christ, to be a witness for Him. Yet we are not supposed to be *of* the world (John 17:16-18).

The difficulty comes in discerning how far *in* we need to be in order to accomplish the purpose for which we have committed our lives and how far we need to stay *not of* the world in order to prevent the associations of which Scripture has forbidden us to partake. Many organizations should be examined in this light. For the sake of our discussion, these are civic clubs, professional associations, honor societies, country clubs, political groups, travel clubs, lodges, and military service related groups. Over a period of years I have belonged to most of these types at one time or another, for various reasons. From these experiences I've decided on some basic ground rules which can be helpful to you in making a decision as to whether or not you as a Christian can afford such an involvement.

1. Is this association necessary? Is it needed for your professional preparedness or for functioning and working in your particular profession or in your particular hobbies or interests?

If others involved in this association are basically non-Christians and if membership serves no other purpose than fellowshipping with non-Christians just for fellowship's sake, such an association would certainly be questionable. "He that walketh with wise men shall be wise: but a companion of fools shall be destroyed" (Prov. 13:20).

2. Does it give opportunity to witness? If the activities of the group are such that they provide no opportunity for witness or no opportunity for people to see you and desire to know about the Gospel, and there are no other specific benefits to be derived from the association, these facts should raise a question as to whether you should join.

3. Is the club's reputation sufficiently neutral? If there are secret ceremonies involved, or if compromising activities are required, or if the general public image of the group is such that even the world might be "surprised" that you as a Christian would be involved in such an organization, your involvement could become a real stumbling block to others and you should consider carefully such involvement. Paul spoke clearly to this issue: "Be ye not unequally yoked together with unbelievers: for what fellowship hath righteousness with unrighteousness? and what communion hath light with darkness?" (2 Cor. 6:14)

4. Does it detract from devotions or witnessing? This question does not imply that time consumption in itself is necessarily bad. There are many occasions where it may be good for relaxation or recreation but if time consumption takes on such proportions that it begins to infringe on the time available for maintaining your spiritual life, then it can become a real problem for a Christian and serious questions should be raised about continuing.

I am not either condemning or sanctioning any specific organization or activity. I know personally many dedicated Christians who are members of country clubs, and who are involved in golf and recreation at these clubs. I see no problem in such involvement if the guidelines above are followed. If it is primarily recreation, if it provides an opportunity to witness, if the image of that specific organization is not too negative, and if it does not become a time problem, the association should not be harmful.

In business it often becomes necessary to be involved in meetings, conferences, and luncheons where there is heavy drinking. This, too, becomes a matter for individual analysis and individual decision. There are situations when this can be handled without compromise; yet there are other times when to continue such an association might seriously harm the cause of Christ and your witness for Him.

I had to make such a decision five years ago when I resigned from a high executive position in the business world. A lower level position in business would not have created such a problem but in the position which I held, to be effective in it in the way in which my superiors expected me to be, seemed to necessitate a deeper involvement in off-hour associations and activities in which I felt I did not want to participate. Rather than be an embarrassment by not following through on these various associations, I chose to back out completely and follow another avenue of work. It has been clear since that time that even in this the Lord was leading by placing that intolerable situation before me so that I would move in the direction He had planned for me.

Clubs and societies are not necessarily bad. Nor are they necessarily good. It depends entirely on the particular organization, the particular circumstances, your relationship to it, and how it affects you and your relationship to Christ.

28

Satan's Filthy Lucre?
Or God's Riches?

There are few subjects in the Bible on which we are given more warning than on our attitude toward money and riches. Many examples are given concerning the downfall of those who have sought after seemingly illusive material gain. Today the desire and pursuit of money and riches, by whatever means, and the use of money for devious purposes seem to be the scourge of society. If in some way the effect of this driving urge to get and to keep money could be removed from our society, it would completely revolutionize our lives. "For the love of money is the root of all evil: which while some coveted after, they have erred from the faith, and pierced themselves through with many sorrows" (1 Tim. 6:10).

But it can't be removed. And it shouldn't be removed. Money, after all, is only a medium of exchange. In its simplest concept money is a piece of paper or a small chunk of metal which represents the labor of someone somewhere at sometime. The basic problem with money is that human nature has basically a master-slave orientation. We all want to acquire the labor of other people, or the medium of exchange which will buy that labor, while at the same time minimizing the amount of labor that we, ourselves, must perform to earn the use of another's services. The higher the wages we demand for our own services, the more services we think we should have in relation to our own.

Look around you. Everything you see, other than the raw land and resources which God placed here on this earth, is the product of the labor of other people. It is essential that we keep the meaning of money and wealth in perspective if we are to adopt a proper Christian view of money and wealth.

Money in itself is not evil. It is, as we have said, a medium of exchange. The problem lies in the love of money, or the pursuit of it in a manner that is not consistent with scriptural principles. If we can keep the view that money is nothing but stored-up labor that is passing through our hands, so that we may enjoy the skills of others while others enjoy the benefits of our skills, and keep in perspective what the Scripture says about material gain, we can avoid the frustrations and ulcers that are associated with money problems.

After all, to a miracle-working God, and to Christians who have the resources and power available to them of this miracle-working God, money certainly shouldn't be a problem. God's Word is very clear on this matter. He has promised to supply all of our needs (Phil. 4:19). He has told us that His blessing makes us rich (Prov. 10:22). He has admonished us in numerous places in the Scripture to avoid seeking after money (1 Tim. 6:10). God has also made it clear that the tithe belongs to Him, the first 10 percent of our income. Beyond that we are challenged to give offerings and to support the work of the Lord.

How much should you give? The answer is simple. You can't outgive God. My dad used to say frequently, "I shoveled out and the Lord shoveled in, but the Lord had a bigger shovel."

Our motive and our attitudes are important in this sense, however. If our purpose for giving to the Lord is to receive a greater blessing or to receive more in return, then our hearts are not right and we cannot expect God to bless. But if our motive is to give to God's work because we love Him and because we want to see His work prosper, then the Lord will recognize that He can trust us with a bountiful supply.

But we must earn that trust. We must demonstrate that trust. Walter Meloon, builder of Correct-Craft Boats, gives testimony of how God took his company through bankruptcy and then later enabled him to pay back every penny that others lost in the bankruptcy, even though he had no legal obligation to do so. In giving his testimony, he sums it up with, "God has no problem with money. He only has a problem with the hearts of men."

When we realize that God has created all of the resources which we have and controls all of the wealth that is available, it's not hard to see the truth of this statement. Yet it seems to be so difficult for Christians to comprehend the meaning of it. My dad was a strong believer in the fact that all of our possessions belong to God if we are trusting in Him. Nothing is ours to control or dispose of as we will. His favorite motto was, "Not how much of my money do I give to the Lord, but how much of the Lord's money do I keep for myself?" To him everything he owned belonged to

God. He treated it that way, and as a result, when God sent vast sums of money his way, it didn't distort his values or his commitment to God's service. Neither did it cause him great disillusionment when several times during his career he himself nearly approached bankruptcy. His reasoning was that if we have given all of what we have to God and then God takes it from us, we should be able to recognize that it was His and not ours and we shouldn't let it disturb our faith and trust in Him when we lose it.

All of this does not mean that we should give everything that we have to a Christian organization or to a church and live in poverty. God expects us to use the money He has entrusted us with as investments for greater return as well. As in the Parable of the Talents (Matt. 25:14-30), He may want us to invest His money for greater returns and use at some future date.

My dad was able to do this to a significant degree during his lifetime. He not only gave large sums of money to the Lord but he committed his entire business to the Lord by giving 90 percent of the stock of his company to a foundation committed to service for the Lord. Thus, any benefits to the business would not flow to him personally but to the Lord's work. As a result God blessed the business greatly and literally millions of dollars were made available for missions and Christian work all over the world.

Let's get the proper perspective on money, what it is, who it belongs to, and how we as Christians should relate to it. Let us put it into the background in our attitudes and goals in life and get on with the job God has given us to do—winning souls for Him while there is yet time.

Conclusion

The values and attitudes set forth in this book on *Success without Compromise* will, I trust, have been of some benefit to you in your Christian experience, whether you have browsed through it independently or studied each chapter carefully in a study group or Sunday School class. The topics, questions, and challenges presented should give you some insights into practical preparation for Christian living from the standpoint of a layman, and should give you a theology and set of values that are helpful, not only in your own Christian living, but in your witnessing and carrying on the work of Christ here on this earth.

What has been presented here has been gleaned from:

1. An earthly father (R. G. LeTourneau) who espoused most, if not all, of the concepts presented herein, and who, in addition to having become a leader in the Christian world, established a reputation as an industrial genius in the manufacturing of earth-moving and construction equipment. In addition, he espoused some concepts in education that are unique, forceful, and which have proved tremendously successful. His influence in transferring this knowledge to the second generation, in a very practical manner, accounts for a great deal of this presentation.

2. A mother, still living and 77 years of age at

this writing, who carried on the home and spiritual training while Dad was so occupied most of the time in business affairs and in Christian witnessing, and who in her own right became the American Mother of the Year in 1969, and who has an extremely practical Christian philosophy of her own, some of which has been revealed in her book, *Recipes for Living*.

3. Over 40 years as a Christian myself, not always in the center of God's will and not always pleasing Him with my actions, but growing through the years, taking note of concepts passed on by my parents, testing them out on my own and then putting them into practice as a Christian layman.

4. Over 25 years in management of business and industry, in management of higher education, and in management and board service on a number of Christian and church organizations. These experiences have helped to develop the concepts of relationships with people and the practical aspects of Christianity both in witnessing and in accomplishing the tasks that are set before us.

Through all of this have been established (1) priorities in life, (2) a rationale for coping with the important issues facing us, (3) a relativity of importance of things and activities, and (4) the importance both of people relations and of accomplishing the purposes and objectives before us in our Christian commitment.

Contrarily it has been brought firmly to our attention, through all of this, the emptiness of knowledge by itself, the emptiness of subsistence-level Christian living, the emptiness of a ritual Christianity, and the emptiness of pleasure as such.

If these discussions have helped in any way in your victorious Christian living, in your accomplishment as a Christian, in your winning others to Christ, in your growth, in your restoration and your stimulation as a vibrant Christian witness, it will all have been worth the time and effort to put it together.

God bless you.